The modern nursery

Longman early childhood education

Cynthia Dawes *Early maths*

David Evans *Sharing Sounds*

Hilda Meers *Helping our children talk*

The modern nursery
Marion Dowling

Longman   London and New York

Longman Group Limited
London and New York
Associated companies, branches and representatives
throughout the world.

© Longman Group Ltd 1976

First published 1976
Second Impression 1978

ISBN 0 582 25004.8 cased edition
ISBN 0 582 25005.6 paper edition

Library of Congress Cataloging in Publication Data

Dowling, Marion.
    The modern nursery.

    (Longman early childhood education series)
    Bibliography: p. 149
    1. Nursery school facilities. I. Title.
LB 3325.N8D68   372.21'6   75-42232
ISBN 0-582-25004-8
ISBN 0-582-25005-6 pbk.

Printed in Great Britain by
Whitstable Litho Ltd., Whitstable, Kent.

Contents

To my husband

Introduction

In the early part of this century Rachel and Margaret McMillan pioneered the first nursery schools in Britain, designed primarily to provide physical and social nurture for young children in deprived urban areas. It is a measure of their dedication and success that some of these schools are still thriving and are the very pillar on which pre-school education has existed over the years.

Despite this, state nursery provision has been pretty well static for the past forty years, and the birth of the playgroup movement in 1961 was the result of a group of mothers determined to establish a self-help group whilst waiting for the government to provide for their under-fives. Now, at last the state has promised more facilities for pre-school children, and already new units for three and four-year-olds are operating.

However thoughts have changed since the first nursery development took place and it is necessary for all concerned with these new nursery projects to analyse just what is going to be provided for our young children. Since the McMillan sisters founded their schools, research has shown that the early years from 0 to 5 are probably the most crucial from an educational point of view. Therefore we clearly need to provide more than social training for the new entrants.

The recent upsurge of interest in early childhood education, the continuing growth of the playgroup movement, and the development and extension of state nursery provision throughout the country make it apparent that there is widespread agreement that these organizations are desirable for young children. The majority of parents are now aware that they should be thinking of arranging some pre-school experience for their child at the age of three or four.

But this certainty about pre-schooling being a 'good thing' becomes rather hazy when adults start to consider *why* it is desirable and even hazier when thoughts turn to what actually happens within the walls of a nursery unit to make it so desirable an experience. Perhaps it would be helpful to consider these basic questions before going any further.

If a parent who is not familiar with nursery provision is asked directly why she wishes to apply for a nursery place for her child she may well reply that 'it will do him good before he goes to school'. A nursery environment is often seen as a gentle means of easing a child into a daily school routine, of enabling him to mix with his peers and giving him experience of other adults whilst weaning him away from home for part of the day. A good nursery environment will ensure that the child does gain all this, and indeed most infant school teachers agree that children who have benefited from nursery or good playgroup experience will have a headstart in confidence and poise at five years. This is important, but to view a nursery education as merely a prelude to school is to have too narrow a vision of this vital time. At approximately three years a child is ready for horizons beyond his immediate home environment, though babyhood is still not far behind. He may still be emotionally unstable: socially he is not able to play in a group situation, his powers of concentration may be non-existent or extremely limited, physically he may still be clumsy and uncoordinated, his curiosity may be insatiable, but linguistically he is still limited in expressing himself. The five-year-old is a sociable being, capable of fluent speech and mastering his emotions for most of the time. He enjoys stories and craft activities and is able to concentrate on producing an end product. Physically he is coordinated and he is developed in gross and finer motor skills.

These early years are critical – the pace of development is rapid in every way and the foundations for learning and living are being laid. This is not just a time for preparing a child for his future schooling, but to aid him to benefit fully from his present stage of development and to equip him for future living.

When we seek to justify nursery education in terms of research findings it must be admitted that data is rather thin and a great deal of work remains to be done in this field. When considering a child's cognitive development, although there is general acceptance that development of intelligence can be and is modified by early experience (Hunt, 1968) it may well be that if nursery education aims to accelerate cognitive learning then a special type of programme needs to be provided and maintained beyond the very short period of nursery schooling. The Headstart programme in America has now found it was over ambitious in expecting an intensive pre-schooling programme to eliminate or mitigate later difficulties in school. Whilst we await new research into the effects and possible benefits of pre-school education, we must beware of expecting too much of what is, after all, generally part-time provision for one or two years of a child's life before he starts his first school. The realization that this is a mere 'drop in the ocean' compared to the time spent at home during the early years has led to concentration on home visiting schemes for the mother and toddler in socially deprived areas, in the hope that parents can be made aware of their role and, with guidance, can be instrumental in purposively aiding their child's development.

Tessa Blackstone (1971) describes the unrealistic expectations of nursery school provision expressed in a 1926 Independent Labour Party pamphlet on nursery schools. This claimed that nursery provision allows for the 'full realisation of the essential human unity in which mind and body cohere', and that 'a working class trained in the nursery school spirit would not tolerate existing conditions, economic or social, and such intolerance is a necessary condition of permanent advance.' In the early years of nursery development the champions of the cause tended to see it as the cure for all ills; it is often necessary for a cause to be overstated in order to achieve results, and the fight for the first nursery schools was a hard one. Today, however, we can look back on 64 years during which some nursery provision has existed in the United Kingdom, and it is now time to examine the hard facts and try to ascertain the justification for this provision.

Quite clearly parents want nursery provision for their children. This is shown by the long waiting lists for all nursery units (it will need an accelerated programme of nursery building to absorb these lists) and the rapid development of the playgroup movement. Some parents, often those in unsuitable housing with inadequate playspace simply need relief from the rigours of child rearing. Many look to the child's needs and realize that they are not capable of providing all that he requires.

Many parents are also suffering from the high standards of child rearing expected today. Our knowledge of children's needs has vastly improved and the mother's role is a demanding one when one views these higher expectations. This, taken in conjunction with urbanization, the mobility of the family and consequent isolation of some young mothers and children in high-rise flats or large housing estates, makes the need for a supportive service for parents and young children apparent. Parenthood is not something that is acquired naturally; it used to be taught informally in the extended family group, today the professionals are intervening where necessary and the nursery school or unit is part of the community service provided for parents to assist them in their task of bringing up their children.

Recent research has shown that the early years are vastly important for predicting later IQ attainment (it is important to differentiate between this and the concept of a fixed IQ). The longitudinal study conducted by the Child Development Bureau showed that by the time a child is seven there are clearly defined differences in levels of attainment between those from different occupational groups. Bloom (1964) states that by five, approximately 50% of a child's final intelligence and 32% of his performance in IQ tests can be predicted. These findings lead us to assume that the years from 0 to 5 are a period of development during which foundations for the future are laid for good or ill. The recent emphasis on the need for pre-schooling programmes to help counteract deprivation lead on from these assumptions. If the nursery can provide a favourable climate for the child during these vulnerable years, working closely with the parent and other community agencies, then some of the effects of disadvantage may be tackled. However, if the benefits of the nursery to disadvantaged children are to be longlasting, the nursery programme does need to be geared to the particular needs of these children.

The White Paper stated in 1972 that 'the extension of nursery education will also provide an opportunity for the earlier identification of children with special difficulties, which if neglected may inhibit their educational progress.' The use of the nursery as a screening device for children is important. Both evidence and commonsense show that if weaknesses such as speech impediments, sight or hearing defects are detected and dealt with early, the problem is often easier to remedy before the child is subjected to the strains of formal schooling. Of course the nursery teacher cannot claim to be an expert in diagnosing all possible difficulties. She will, however, with experience learn to identify the children who are likely to be at risk in the future on the basis of present problems in the nursery. Westman, Rice and Bermann who studied the records of 130 nursery school children and their later school careers found that those with difficulties at nursery school level were likely to have problems later on. They considered that the observations of the nursery teacher were essential to assist with mental health screening.

The final justification for nursery provision is a subjective one, but none the less important. Any observer, trained or untrained, visiting a good playgroup or nursery unit cannot fail to be impressed by the enthusiasm and enjoyment shown by the children. We have presented reasons for considering nursery provision as educationally and socially desirable, even though there has been little proven research on these aspects. It is worth considering the following quotation from Elkind which assists us in making a case for the nursery on the grounds of the pleasure that it provides:

Nursery school experience most assuredly has immediate value for the child to the extent that it helps him to appreciate and enjoy his immediate world to the full, and to better prepare him for future social and intellectual activities . . . isn't it enough that we lighten the burdens of childhood for even a brief period each day without demanding at the same time that we produce permanent results? The contributions of the nursery school . . . do not have to be long-lived to be of value.

We will now turn to that question formulated by many interested parents in varying ways but meaning: 'What will you be teaching my child whilst he is with you for one or two years?' This is a very reasonable question and a very difficult one to answer, because the parent wishes to be reassured that his or her child will be using his time well and acquiring certain skills and amassing useful facts. The nursery teacher knows that if she is doing her job properly the child will be using his time well, but the acquisition of skills and facts is secondary to the development of psychological mechanisms such as perception and cognition, and the growth of a stable and independent personality. So the nursery unit and the adults who work in it have the challenging task of assessing the child as he enters the environment and providing an atmosphere which will enable that child to grow in every sense, equiping him with qualities of confidence, flexibility and emotional stability, which will hold him in good stead for the future.

The curiosity and energy of the three-year-old knows no bounds, his interest in the world around him is limitless. What happens to this enthusiasm and interest in early adolescence? Why are some of these children so bored and so apathetic towards learning? We cannot afford to waste the valuable energies displayed by our pre-school children. We do not have to show a young child *how* to learn, he is busy learning from the moment of birth, but we must nurture and extend this process by encouraging the child to want to learn more: we must *motivate* him. Motivation will not be achieved by a set pattern of instruction or rigid programmed learning: it will only be fostered by providing conditions in the nursery that will strengthen the child's natural wish to learn. (Details of this are in the chapter on activities.)

We must remember however, that as teachers we are not dealing with 'clean sheets of paper': children come to us with three years of home experience, and in an unfavourable home situation a child's natural motivation may well have already been stunted. In an atmosphere of marital stress, where play and freedom and curiosity are discouraged and a child is regarded as at best a nuisance, interest and zest will gradually give way to withdrawn indifference. Then the teacher's role will be to penetrate that indifference and to re-create the enthusiasm for learning. The child whose parents decide to send him to a nursery unit will be sending him for his first experience of the educational system. The parent may also have fears that she is relinquishing her child and placing him into the hands of professionals. These fears should be realized by the teacher, who will make every attempt to reassure the parent. We hear a great deal about home and school cooperation throughout the system: certainly at this early age it is essential that the parent and teacher interact in their roles for the benefit of the child. Susan Isaacs always described the nursery school as 'an extension to the home' — today with the family lives of many children in an unsatisfactory state, the nursery should operate to reinforce what family relationships there are and to strengthen those parents who feel ill equipped to cope with their children — no nursery environment however satisfactory can hope to supplant the role of the parent.

The learning that takes place with the parent in the 'good home' in an atmosphere of affection and security is ideal : the pre-school unit (albeit school, class, playgroup or nursery centre) will attempt to provide some of these elements for the child who does not experience such a home environment. For the more fortunate who do, the unit will aim to build upon already solid foundations, providing an exciting and stimulating series of situations and encouraging the child to make the fullest use of them.

In a *Study of Nursery Education* (Schools Council, 1972) nursery teachers were asked to consider specific aims of nursery education and to place them on a five point scale. Very generally, the overall order of these aims was social, intellectual, home-school relations, aesthetic appreciation and physical skills. When asked to give a personal statement of the aims of educating young children, the majority of teachers gave as their first priority social, emotional and moral development of the individual within himself and in a group situation. These then are the views of a good sample of mature and experienced nursery teachers, and we will accept for our purposes that this is what we hope to achieve with our young children.

Going back to the parent, it remains difficult to explain the 'educative' part of nursery education, particularly when a nursery environment shows a group of children apparently 'just playing', often with very messy materials, often making a great deal of noise, and often apparently doing nothing. Any visitor can see that this group of children are happy, but what are they doing ? Vera Roberts, an experienced nursery headteacher, describes what she sees to be happening to her children in a practical situation :

I put emotional security in a wide circle first because this is essential for full development. . . . His social development is promoted by his play with other young children . . . through role play he learns who he is, who others are, and what it feels like to be them. Intellectual growth is encouraged by the stimulating environment in which he is led to observe, to experiment, to question, to discuss. He learns how to learn rather than accumulating a number of facts. Through free experimentation with materials he builds up a body of experience from which to form adequate concepts : by talking and listening he develops his language ability.

Essentially then, a child's development will not progress satisfactorily unless he is given the opportunity to explore and experiment in order to grow to understand his environment. Piaget above all others has been instrumental in showing us the essential connection between these activities and the child learning. Moreover, however lavish and well equipped a nursery environment, its success will depend on the skill of the adults working there in involving the child and motivating him to continue learning.

This book attempts to trace various aspects of nursery policy and practice, but the strongest argument put forward is for the pre-school unit to work within a community context. The Plowden Report was the first to crystallize former beliefs about the importance of home-school liaison, and although early nursery provision involved some measure of contact with the mothers, today with the mobility of labour, a growing immigrant population and one-parent families the need is even greater and more complex. The welfare state means that a large group of health visitors, social and welfare workers are operating in the community for the benefit of the young child and his family, and yet there is still a hard core of social deprivation which is not being served by these workers. A certain type of nursery provision aimed at such deprived groups may start to infiltrate and attack social disadvantage, but it is not enough to follow the old traditional school pattern. The nursery teacher's role has changed and widened in scope as has that of the nursery nurse. Attention is being focused on the necessity for a child to have fluent mastery of his language in order for him to succeed in the school system. This has inevitably brought up the issue of whether structured language schemes should be introduced at pre-school level. It is important to give thought to these different policies in order to make nursery provision relevant to the individual child.

Many headteachers faced with new nursery units, and newly trained teachers are very naturally looking for some guidelines on how to develop and run these establishments for young children: it is hoped that this book will give some guidance on the organization of the nursery within the administrative and social framework. We also recognize that young childrens' needs are being met in a variety of ways at this time by both trained and untrained personnel. Throughout the book I have stressed the interdependent development of children and as the implications of this interdependence are recognized, the argument about who does what job will, I hope, lessen. Caring for and educating the child become indistinguishable, and the more we all learn about everything which affects young children and their growth then the greater hope for their future. In this spirit the book is offered to anyone who will find it helpful.

There is present confusion about terminology when talking about establishments for young children. State nursery classes and nursery schools are provided by the Department of Education : most day nurseries are the responsibility of the Department of Health and Social Security, and nursery centres are a hybrid result of joint provision from both departments. In the private sector playgroups, private nursery groups and childminders are the responsibility of Social Services. All these cater for the pre-school child, and even the term 'pre-school' is now questioned, as nursery classes are attached to primary schools and as both they and nursery schools are equipped and staffed in the same way as any other educational establishment.

In order to overcome this confusion, I have used the term 'young child' to describe any child between two and five years. This is the age when he is most likely to attend one of the above establishments, although day nurseries, some nursery centres and childminders will take children from 0 to 5 years, and most playgroups and all nursery classes will only accept children over three years.

I have also used the term 'nursery unit' throughout the book (with the exception of some discussion in the last section) and am primarily thinking of practice in state nursery classes and schools. However, this practice is equally relevant for any adult dealing with this age group. In the same way I refer throughout to the 'teacher', but this term is used loosely to refer to the adult with the child at that moment.

Finally, I realize that, after reading this book, many teachers will feel that I am asking the impossible of them, and students will be disheartened at the magnitude of their future job. Many of my suggestions for community involvement require dedication from the practitioner, and there will be very few, if any nursery units where all of these suggestions can be carried out simultaneously. I remain unconvinced that there is any less reason for stating a case for them. All adults concerned with young children should be thinking people, and if the suggestions stimulate thought and consequently some action, then this is achievement enough.

Part one   The modern nursery unit

1
Planning and providing

THE NURSERY ON PAPER

How many times have we entered new buildings to hear groans from the staff working in them – the comments are the same whether it is a block of offices, a hospital or a school – 'if only the architects had consulted us before building' or 'it looked all right on paper but it just doesn't work out in bricks and mortar'. This is very fair comment. Sometimes the planners have completed their part of the job and the builders are implementing the plans before it is realized all too late that something essential to the practical situation has been neglected. More often than not the completed shiny building looks beautiful empty but when filled with busy hospital staff or a group of children it becomes clear that the paper thin walls are just not sufficient for the required privacy or the absorption of noise.

If we are not careful the same thing will happen with the new nursery provision. In many schools existing classrooms have been converted and a nursery class developed with only minor alterations to cloakroom and toilet facilities. In other areas elaborate nursery schools or even nursery centres with multiple pre-school provision are being built. In all cases it is essential that the headteacher of the school is consulted at the earliest possible opportunity and brought in to consider the plans from the moment they emerge. However, this will be of little use unless the head can make some positive contributions at the planning stage, and this many feel unqualified to do as they have had no experience of working in a modern nursery setting. Visits to other new nurseries are useful, but as yet these are few and far between.

The main criteria to be considered in a nursery building are safety – both from health hazards and physical dangers ; a reassuring environment that is welcoming to both parent and child ; and one that challenges and excites children in a way that will promote their all-round development. This first chapter is an attempt to offer help to the teacher who is faced with the prospect of a new nursery, but feels ill-prepared to state her demands as to building or equipment. It is not designed to depict the ideal nursery but to suggest some salient points that are worth remembering when working with small children in modern conditions. The requirements are basic to a nursery unit attached to a primary school or to a separate nursery school.

The playroom should be as large as the financial grant will allow – maximum space should be a number one priority. If sliding partitions are fitted, the room can then be split up as desired, into as many as four different areas if necessary to allow for quiet activities or music or using the full floor space on a wet day when physical activities can be provided inside. Alternatively the room can be arranged as one large central area surrounded by a number of small bays where the children may withdraw into small groups at will – these may be divided off by curtains or sliding screens.

It is worth considering the entire volume of space in the playroom rather than just the floor area. A 'crow's nest' in a corner provides an ideal den for children – it can simply comprise a platform on stilts with a ladder leading up to it – if desired the platform can be extended along the length of one wall to provide a gallery. It is important that the platform is left open – any attempt to create a covered house will allow the children to be cut off from the adults and the value of language development will be lost to the teacher. This is worth noting throughout the nursery. The children should certainly be allowed an illusion of privacy whilst still under observation by the adult in charge. In this way their free play may be expanded and developed, and a dimension of structure added if required.

An attractive setting is important, and this means lots of colour and texture carefully used. Many young children do lead a colourless existence in homes where priority has to be given to the essentials of life. This group in particular, usually from areas of social deprivation, need to experience something of beauty at school. Walls in glowing colours and warm, carpeted areas for the book corner will help to meet this need. Interesting wall surfaces could be requested such as hessian, cork or stone; even bare bricks or plaster in a small area will provide good tactile experience for small hands. The playroom will need to be divided into different areas and this is helped by the use of various colours, wall textures and floor levels. Flexibility is advisable however and it is not a good idea to paper the 'home corner' area with kitchen type wallpaper as one might well want to change this arrangement in the future. Neutral shades are often just as attractive as strong colours and will help to create an illusion of space where provision has not been overgenerous. Everything possible should be done to create interest in what is often a conventional box shaped area.

Practicability is also important – where possible wall coverings should be washable and a messy play space can be attractively separated from the rest of the room by being on a slightly lower level with an extra practical floor covering. This covering should be resistant to paint and water — many are not in older nurseries and polythene sheets have to be carefully laid down daily to protect surfaces. Quarry tiles have been found most practical for messy play although they are expensive.

If possible there should be a small area or room near the playroom which can be isolated for special sessions with individual children - often behaviour difficulties require a one-to-one relationship with an adult in a quiet atmosphere. Other children will require individual attention for language development. This area need not be large but again it should be attractively furnished and welcoming to the child.

If the building is to be a separate nursery school there will be a minimum of two playrooms. It is a good idea for these rooms to vary somewhat in design to provide for varying needs. Normally a nursery school will allow children to wander from room to room for at least part of the day, and a different layout in each room will create interest and make different presentation of activities possible. One room may consist of several small bays whilst the other may provide more central space, and this is the room that will be used for physical play during wet weather.

A school should also have provision for a school office and a staff room which may double up as a parents' room. This may appear to be labouring an obvious point — however, in the past architects have looked at the relatively small numbers of children being admitted to nursery schools (rarely more than the equivalent of 60 full-time children) and decided that anything more than one all-purpose room for adults was extravagant. This just isn't so. Clearly a school secretary must have a room in which to see to the school's administrative work, and the headteacher would normally share this when seeing parents (sometimes privacy is required when talking to families and then an alternative room must be found). An adult working in a nursery environment does need to have a proper rest during the day, and this should be taken away from the children — at other times of the day this staff room could be used for the many community projects that the nursery may be involved in and which are mentioned later in the book.

Laundry facilities are also important in an independent unit — gone are the days when all towels and flannels were boiled weekly as disposables are now used. However, children of three and four do need clean pants from time to time and a drying machine is a must. A higher standard of hygiene should be aimed at than that required for older children. Dressing up clothes need to be washed regularly and all hats disinfected — the younger the child the more vulnerable he is to infection.

A separate nursery school will be entitled to its own kitchen if it is to admit full-time children. An attached nursery unit would share the

4

facilities of the main school, but if at all possible they should be allowed a small servery to enable meals sent from the main kitchen to be served in the nursery. The midday meal is a most vulnerable time of day — particularly for a small child — and to expect children of nursery age to eat in a large dining hall with older children is unreasonable. The servery in the nursery unit should contain an oven to allow the children to do their own cookery activities (using the main kitchen for this is not satisfactory as the children need to be made aware of how things are cooked).

Children's lavatories and washbasins should adjoin the playroom and the lavatories should be fitted with half-doors to ensure a measure of privacy, but to allow the adult access if necessary. Washbasins should be at the height of the small child and some form of sluice should be fitted with a hand shower attachment. This will allow a dirty child to be washed thoroughly and any soiled matter to be rinsed away.

Pre-school equipment is generally bulky and this should be considered when planning storage space. A large walk-in stock cupboard and an outside shed for large physical apparatus and wheeled toys are the minimum requirements for every nursery playroom.

All these points need to be considered in any type of nursery provision. Careful initial thought may prevent considerable frustration later on. It is also worth noting that different emphasis on needs should be considered according to the type of area that the unit or school is going to serve. A building designed for an E.P.A. locality will require more laundry facilities, extra accommodation for parents and a larger outside area than a school serving children from a garden suburb. In general our ruling must be the more deprived the child, the more generous the provision for him.

WHAT SHALL I ORDER?

Visitors to a nursery unit will usually be struck by a number of young children engrossed in their play; in groups, singly or with adults these children are pouring themselves into their activities: absorbed in book or painting corners, busy in home corners, or rushing around in more vigorous dramatic play, children are responding to the environment they are in. The quality of the children's play will only be as good as the environment provided for them. This environment develops from the equipment and materials provided and the way in which these are presented and organized by the adults in the nursery. An environment designed only to allow the children a safe place in which to play will lead to restricted activities, as many exciting materials have an element of risk about them. (One could refuse to have sand in a nursery because of the danger of it being thrown: climbing frames involve the risk of a fall and woodwork activity the risk of a cut.) Equipment should be sufficiently challenging to the child, and the adult is there to aid each individual to use it properly and to learn correct techniques in use. Therefore, sand should be allowed with the simple rule of 'no throwing because it is dangerous'; climbing frames will be used according to each child's capability, but they will grow to understand that pushing someone on a frame could lead to an accident; woodwork should always be supervised subtly by an adult who should make sure that children can handle their tools properly. Generally, teaching safe use of equipment is a more positive approach than banning it because of possible danger.

The equipment is an important part of the nursery and when one looks at an initial allowance and then at the vast range of equipment displayed in pre-school catalogues it becomes apparent that selectiveness is necessary. A great deal can be done to compensate for inadequate allowances by improvising and making equipment out of second hand materials – the word 'compensate' is probably not a good one because every work situation for small children should include a good measure of home-made equipment. If the adult uses her initiative and demonstrates how familiar objects such as buttons and egg boxes can be used for sorting, or a clothes horse with a curtain can become a tent, this will encourage the children to be lively minded and adapt materials for themselves.

Just what do we provide in a nursery to enable our young children to get the greatest possible benefits from their one or two years in such a setting? We are thinking of 'gains' in terms of social, emotional, physical and intellectual progress and so our requests for equipment must centre on enabling these developments to take place. Susan Isaacs says that 'children need freedom and choice if they are to grow up responsible and independent beings. They learn to exercise responsibility by having it.' Our choice of equipment must reflect the child's need to develop independently: easily accessible toilets eliminate the necessity of the child asking the adult every time he wishes to use the lavatory; open-sided storage units with low shelves filled with jigsaws, construction toys or art materials allow the child to select what he requires, and with the encouragement of an adult to return the items to where they belong; double sinks with a wide draining board area allow the children to organize their own source of water-play, and provides them with a suitable area for washing up their own paintpots at the end of the day. Young children have no wish to be dependent – if they are given the opportunity to be self-sufficient they quickly become adept, and revel in their newly found skills, taking great pleasure in teaching them to the younger and less able children. This developing self-confidence will stand them in good stead for the future.

When deciding what play facilities should be provided initially in a new nursery unit, the answer must be that messy play should be a priority because this type of activity is so bound up with all facets of development in young children. Emotional needs are particularly satisfied through this play, and many temper tantrums, fears and inhibitions will be resolved in a group situation. Wet and dry sand, water, dough, clay and paint should all be provided in ingenious ways. Sand and water trays, painting easels and solid tables for clay and dough should be some of the first orders for the nursery. Messy play is extremely difficult for even the most dedicated mother to provide at home, particularly if home conditions are small and cramped. If the school can give the child early experience of these materials sound foundations for learning will be laid: the child will bang out his aggressions on the clay, will be soothed and fascinated by the properties of water and sand, and will wallow in the colour and texture of painting and the various painting techniques that are suitable for this age group. Basic instincts will be satisfied and the beginnings of creativity will be developed.

Various needs are satisfied by imaginative play. Children do need to take on varying roles in order to come to terms with the world around them. Fantasies will be played out daily and one of the important areas for this is the home corner. As mentioned previously this should not be too enclosed or limited in size. It should also be capable of being transformed into a hospital, dental surgery, hairdresser's or shop and suitable props should be chosen with this in mind. These should be made available as the moment arises and can be quite simple – a steering wheel on a stand and a line of chairs will serve excellently as a bus, fire engine or aeroplane. A large tractor inner tube can be a boat, can encircle an imaginary lake or can just be an enjoyable 'bouncer'. Planks, ramps and boxes are a good means of providing for the child's physical needs to balance and climb, and yet these will also adapt as equipment for elaborate imaginative activities.

Social development partly means learning to be one of a group – concepts of sharing, adapting and taking one's turn have to be learned and much of this takes place in group activities. Joint projects in creative work, cookery groups and imaginative and physical group play will develop this awareness of others. It follows that any initial equipment for the nursery should be purchased with a view to using it jointly. Hidey holes, climbing frames, sandpits are all made for cooperative ventures, while swings and wheeled toys are more likely to promote solitary play and are of secondary importance.

Finally when looking at commercial products for the nursery three things should be born in mind. The first should be the need for change. Needs and methods in education are subject to change, and although a teacher should have some clear vision as to aims there should always be room for experimentation. Buildings should be able to adapt to different methods. This points to having few fixtures in rooms and moveable pieces of furniture which can be grouped to provide quiet corners and play areas. Gone are the days of 'Wendy Houses' which could only accommodate two or three children with difficulty and were terrifyingly flimsy. Bookcases and storage units can divide a home corner off effectively, providing more space and, again, allowing access for the adult.

The second consideration should be strength. Young children have abundant energy and enthusiasm and these qualities are used when they play. Strength is a prerequisite of any piece of equipment used in a nursery and usually the simpler the design the stronger the equipment. If possible, nothing should be ordered from a catalogue without first seeing the equipment in use and hearing how well it has withstood wear and tear. Photographs can give an illusion of solidity, hiding the fact that only thin plywood has been used in manufacture. Most sturdy equipment is made in wood, although new items such as slides and hidey holes made from fibreglass are virtually indestructible.

Thirdly each piece of apparatus must be considered to see what dimensions of play it offers to the children. Ideally equipment should be capable of being used for various types of play, according to the children's own powers of creativity. A climbing frame can be used as a substitute for a tree or it can be a house, or a ship or a series of climbing steps for small feet. Often the simpler the equipment the greater the possibilities it offers for play.

THE NURSERY GARDEN

Children seek access to a place where they can dig in the earth, build huts and dens with timber, use real tools, experiment with fire and water, take really great risks and learn to overcome them. They want a place where they can create and destroy, where they can build their own worlds, with their own skills, at their own time, and in their own way. In our built-up towns, they never find these opportunities. They're frustrated at every turn or tidied out of existence. (Lady Allen of Hurtwood, 1965)

Outdoor facilities in a nursery are assuming an even greater importance as open space is generally becoming more and more limited for children. Children of nursery age do need space to run freely, to dig, climb and potter and to make a mess – all these activities give intense pleasure. They are also necessary food for growth.

Families living in small, modern houses are provided with tiny pocket handkerchief sized gardens – no facilities for children are allowed here amidst neat rows of flowers and tidy lawns. Flat dwellers do not even have this, they have to rely on the public parks or playgrounds which so often consist of a boring piece of asphalt – sometimes with roundabouts, swings and a slide dotted about. School play facilities for many children are just as bad: unimaginative, asphalt rectangles completely barren, except for the netball markings and netball posts. No wonder there are constant fights, incredible noise and sometimes a reluctance on the part of schoolchildren 'to go out to play' when one sees just what they are going out to play on. Rural children are faring little better. Today open countryside is becoming increasingly rare and certainly in the south of England the land is so intensively farmed that children no longer have any place to roam. These children do not even have a park nearby to compensate, only the threat of encroaching housing estates and growing suburbia.

The outdoor space in the nursery should be designed to help fill the need of our young children – where the local environment has failed to make provision for space and all that goes with it the school must provide. The outdoor area allotted to a nursery will vary considerably, but attention should be paid to at least some of the following points when planning this part of the setting.

Safety and seclusion must be first considerations. A nursery play area must be fenced off from any vehicle entrance to the school, and any entrances leading to the road must have safety hooks attached. An attached nursery unit should have its own garden area separated from the main playground and ideally the garden should have a southerly aspect to allow for shelter and the fullest possible use of the site.

A flat area of grass may be provided where the children can picnic in the summer and have room to run freely – this is particularly important for children from a crowded urban environment. This flat area should be varied with small hillocks to allow for different levels on which to play – things look different when viewed from a different height, and undulating ground will always provide an element of surprise for the child and is an excellent base for 'hide-and-seek'. There also needs to be a generously paved area for wetter weather when it is not so convenient to use the grass. This paved space should be large enough to use wheeled toys.

If a new site is being prepared, any trees should be carefully conserved – no amount of expensive climbing frames and swings will compensate for a low branched tree where the children may climb and have ropes and tyres suspended for swinging. If one is lucky enough to have a suitable tree, a small platform or house erected in the branches will give untold delight. Even if a site is treeless, young ones may be planted. One or two felled tree trunks transported to the garden will allow further climbing and imaginative activities.

Most children are not allowed to dig properly in their own garden at home – a plot for digging at school will give great satisfaction, unlike a sandpit children will find that their earth plot is apparently bottomless, and many treasures will be discovered during their work in the way of worms, spiders and other insects. A good sized sandpit with a surrounding paved area is a necessity, preferably situated near to another pit as children do like to be able to dump their sand somewhere. Any shallow stream or pond should be preserved; if wellington boots are the order of the day, children can wade, float twigs, mix earth and water, or, on a warm day, just paddle.

Some part of the nursery garden should be wild: even children living in residential areas with generous gardens, or near to parks miss the real gifts of nature – ability to ramble through weeds, to pick wild flowers at will and curl up unobserved in a tangle of undergrowth. Neat flowerbeds and tidy paths will not fulfil these needs. The 'wild' area need not be large, it could contain several shrubs which attract insects – a hardy buddleia will lure many types of butterflies to the area – grass could be allowed to grow long and one or two boulders could provide climbing targets. This part of the garden will be where the more adventurous children gather – it will be a place to explore and for imaginative projects to start.

Pathways are exciting to a small child – they can be followed, and they lead somewhere. Narrow winding paths should be laid in the garden and as much use as possible made of different surfacing. A cobbled path of rounded pebbles, a track made from ashes or from crazy paving all provide visual interest and feel different to small feet.

Animals

A nursery should have animals, but only if the teacher is fully aware of their needs and the livestock are made a valuable part of the teaching environment. Pets need to be hardy, reasonably easy to handle and easy to transport to temporary homes during school holidays. The most suitable animals to keep indoors are mice, rats, gerbils, hamsters and various insects and reptiles in a vivarium. Outside, rabbits, guinea pigs, chickens and tortoises can be kept quite easily. These should be accommodated in good size hutches and runs, and the children should be encouraged to help feed and clean them out. This helps them develop a sense of responsibility, and as most of these animals have fairly short lives, children can have their first introduction to death when a school pet dies.

As indoors, areas need to be provided for different activities and this will determine where equipment and fixtures are to be situated. Let us look briefly at some of the areas most beneficial for the children.

Building area

Brick play can be most constructive indoors, but nothing can compare with the satisfaction of building a real 'den' in the garden. A three sided shelter is an ideal place for a wood pile where planks, blocks and sticks for outside building can be stored. If the shelter is large enough the children may work here even in wet weather – building is vigorous work and absorbs inexhaustible energies.

Physical play area

This should be situated around any suitable trees – ropes, planks, tyres and slides may be arranged in varying ways to allow children to climb, balance, jump and swing, all necessary to muscle development and development of confidence. Much of this apparatus can be acquired cheaply – this is another example of where improvised materials lead to the children using their imagination in their play – rather than the teacher purchasing expensive slides and swings which can only be used in a limited way.

Area for relaxation

It is important to make provision for the child who does not wish to be very active all the time – most children have a natural rhythm of work and after very vigorous activity will wish to rest for a time. Small seats in a sheltered area will allow for this – logs cemented into the ground make excellent stools and a wooden bench under a tree will be welcomed by some of the quieter members of the group.

Outdoor area for 'indoor' activities

If part of the paved area near to the building is covered to form a type of open veranda, it makes it quite possible to bring sand, water, paint and carpentry outside in all but the worst weather. By using the outside area as an extension of the playroom more messy activities may be used. All forms of play should be made available to the children whatever the weather – in very wet weather, climbing apparatus should come into the playroom, and during the warmer months most of the indoor apparatus can be taken outside.

Outside space is precious and should be used to the full – the nursery garden is not just a place to be visited for fifteen minutes a day, nor is it to be kept solely for the summer months. Arthur Gilbert, who has a nursery school in New York, describes their use of the garden:

Experience of past winters alerts us to the special delights and opportunities they offer. We anticipate some ice skating if there is an extended cold snap. We have the opportunity to see how the streams look when they are almost frozen over. Sun and snow make a variety of sights and pleasures. We always make snowmen. Thawing days are special. Few streams can equal the kinds made by sun, mushy snow and curious children. It does get messy, but oh, what glorious messiness.

2
The adults in the nursery

Modern buildings are a nice bonus – they do ease our daily routine and can help an environment to look attractive and fresh. The atmosphere inside the building, however, is not a matter of bricks and mortar and only the adults working there can decide the policy that will affect the child for good or ill. Much of the teaching nowadays at primary level is a matter of team work. In the nursery unit a team approach is essential. If the unit is a separate nursery school then it is likely to be small (usually not more than the equivalent of 60 full-time places). The children are likely to come into close contact with all members of staff; domestic, administrative and teaching. Such an intimate atmosphere demands that all adults have a good relationship among themselves and a common approach to the children. If the unit is attached to a primary school it will be the responsibility of the class teacher and her nursery nurse and this again is another team situation. In this case care must be taken to see that the needs of the nursery children are carefully balanced with the needs of the rest of the school, and this requires that the nursery teacher has close liaison with her colleagues.

We will now explore the differing roles of the adults employed to work in the nursery situation. The part played by parents and other visitors is acknowledged to be important and will be followed up in the section on the community.

THE NURSERY STAFF

The nursery teacher
The fact that growth and development take place so rapidly during these early years means that only adults of the highest calibre and sensitivity should be selected for nursery teachers – let us immediately get rid of the idea that nursery teachers are infant teachers writ small, or that their only expertise needs to be in childminding. One of the frustrations for the primary and nursery teacher is their lack of status compared to that accorded to secondary and grammar school teachers. This has been present throughout the development of our educational

system and is partly due to the inadequate pupil/teacher system of training primary school teachers which lasted until the beginning of this century. Although a three year teacher training course has been in existence since 1960 for all secondary and primary teachers, and now many in the primary field are taking their B.Ed. we do need to have a degree course established in Early Childhood Education to provide training in sufficient depth, and with a certain prestige to attract students of the necessary calibre.

Traditionally, nursery teachers have been women. The job is particularly attractive to women who marry and have a family and wish to return part time or full time to their former career. This convenience aspect is sometimes more important to a woman than the prospect of commanding a higher salary or promotion in the job. This lack of expectation has contributed to the poor financial rewards and inadequate career structure for teachers of young children. (In the nursery school of course career prospects have been almost non-existent in the past because there have been so few nursery schools and classes.) This combination of traditional staffing of nursery units, together with low status and poor career prospects has meant that a post in a nursery unit has not been an attractive proposition for most men. This is understandable but unfortunate in so far as a man has a very definite role to play in the nursery environment. The National Child Development Bureau study says that 'the conclusion seems warranted that boys in general and working class boys in particular are at higher risk at the primary school stage in terms of their emotional and social adjustment.' It may be that small boys experience difficulties at school because it is a female orientated world. A teacher's approval is usually shown of oral and reading skills and again the child development study finds that boys are more often behind in this facet of development. Boys tend to be less compliant in a classroom situation and more prone to outbursts of physical agression. Although this is recognized as part and parcel of the child's development such behaviour is possibly less well received or tolerated by a woman teacher than a man.

Marital breakup and illegitimacy are becoming more frequent and many children are left without a father in the home. The presence of a man in the nursery environment could do a great deal to redress the balance during these formative years. It is to be hoped that future career prospects and status of nursery teachers will increase with the expansion of the profession, and more men will be encouraged to enter this field of education.

What characteristics do we look for in a 'good' nursery teacher? A person who is a successful teacher, who is able to understand the needs of small children and relate to them and who can form sound relationships with other adults would probably combine all the desired qualities. The first requirement of a successful teacher is to establish herself as a leader and have a degree of rapport with her pupils. R S Peters in *Ethics and Education* comments that 'the ability to form and maintain relationships is almost a necessary condition of doing anything else in a manner that is not warped or stunted.' The development of a good personal relationship as an educational aim usually means that the teacher should have personal relationships with her children, and that the children should learn to form personal relationships both in the nursery and in preparation for future life. The socializing process is one of the pivots of nursery education.

The teacher's particular contribution to her group lies in the nature of her personality. It is impossible to specify the ideal personality to work with young children as every individual has her strengths and weaknesses. A young exuberant probationer will romp with the children and her enthusiasm and energy will be infectious to a group. An older and more experienced, though calmer, personality will create a sense of confidence in her group and will provide the required mother substitute figure for the small newcomer. It is important for the teacher to remember that her group of children are being greatly influenced by her. A child of three or four is still at the imitative stage in his development and his teacher becomes the most important person to him next to his parents. Thus, whatever attitudes and prejudices are shown by the teacher, they will be mirrored by her children. This responsibility should not be taken lightly.

The good teacher must establish herself as effective in the art of teaching, and this brings us to the question of what the children should be learning in the nursery. In the Schools Council study of nursery education the teachers concerned were asked to rate the importance of certain educational objectives for putting the aims of nursery education into practice. Broadly speaking, those listed as most important were the social and communicative skills. Next came the personal controls, development of physical skills and rational objectives, and last came the reasoning and aesthetic objectives together with health and hygiene. The teachers did not consider that learning formal skills merited an important place in the nursery curriculum. This may seem to contradict the original stated aims of nursery education; one of which was intellectual development. In fact the teachers probably stress this part of development in terms of *motivation*. Above all else a teacher must assist the children to want to learn and acquisition of formal skills is only a tiny fragment of this aim. To ensure that her group of children really are learning and that the environment is truly progressive, the teacher of young children must have a good knowledge of child development. She must assess the stage of development that each child has reached upon entry to the nursery, and his consequent progression. The teacher will, moreover, be responsible for planning overall policy for the children in the unit and for keeping a simple record of their development. Record keeping can be very time consuming and time is precious in a nursery day; one suggestion is that the teacher keeps a loose leaf folder or notebook for her group of children, allowing a page for each child. Any relevant information about the child can be jotted down as it becomes available – it may be facts from the family or simply his development at school. By the end of the child's nursery career a composite history has been compiled, though it will not have been necessary for all this information to be placed in permanent form on a record card. However, record cards are important if there is to be maximum benefit from the progress that has taken place during these early years. As these cards are to be handed on to a teacher who has no previous knowledge of the child it will be necessary to sift the information obtained during the year and to transfer only facts that will aid the child in his new class. This last point is essential because of the danger of successive teachers forming preconceptions about the child on the strength of his record card. (See Appendix B on Record-keeping.)

The Schools Council study of nursery education placed communicative skills as one of their highest objectives for the young child and indeed language development is now generally regarded as the most important of the tools that the child must acquire for his future development. Dr Joan Tough says that 'for the disadvantaged child the teacher may be the only person he will meet who can promote the development of new uses of language, who can help him to see that communication of his ideas is worthwhile.' Although structured language kits have been tried and are being used in some educational priority areas, Dr Tough recommends that language learning situations should generally be introduced during the normal pattern of daily activity. Thus the teacher's relationship with the individual child is once again emphasized. It is through this relationship that she will ensure that each child is encouraged to think clearly for himself and that he learns to use language as a means of expressing these thoughts in a logical fashion.

This brings us to the second requirement for a 'good' nursery teacher – her ability to relate to young children and to establish an environment conducive to their needs. Alice Yardley comments that the hallmark of a good teacher is that she is able to put the childrens' interests before her own. This is an important point and it does mean that the teacher should have developed a degree of self-awareness and made some effort to understand and deal with her own problems. Until she has sorted herself out she will be of little use to others, and particularly unsuitable to young children, who will be at the most vulnerable time in their lives. Perhaps this points to the wisdom of having a nucleus of more mature nursery teachers. In *The Role of the Teacher in the Nursery and Infant School*, Joan Cass observes just how often the young, inexperienced teacher is put in charge of the youngest group of children in the school. She goes on to say:

We pay lip service to the fact that the years under five are the most formative and vital period in a child's whole life and yet we often put them in the sole charge of adults or adolescents who know little about the deeper needs and problems of childhood and are still in the process of trying to cope with their own difficulties.

The nursery teacher should have patience and an unhurried approach to the working day. Small children should work at their own pace, and as far as possible should not be forced to fit into a rigid daily timetable. The mode of day should be determined by the children's motivation and their teacher should go along with this, abandoning projects when they are not developed and providing material and resources for expansion when the children express an interest in a theme. Many three and four-year-olds from disadvantaged homes will find it difficult to hold even the simplest conversation; most are unable to take part in any group activity when first entering the nursery and no young child is able to sit still for long. The teacher of such a group cannot afford to take anything for granted and Miss Cass observes that the more experienced and secure teacher tends to make less demands on the children and pays less attention to such things as outward order and tidiness, concentrating more on the child's individual needs. To work in this way and to be prepared to adapt demands a degree of flexibility not required for those working with older age groups. Finally a nursery teacher must be physically fit. As we have mentioned previously, children in a nursery will want to use outdoor premises as an extension of their playroom, and at least one adult should be in the garden with them whenever the weather permits. The ceaseless energy and enthusiasm of small children is a delight but very exhausting. It is impossible to 'switch-off' in a nursery environment and if the admission policy is for full-time and part-time children the rest time for the adult during the working day can only be brief. Stamina and energy are prerequisites for all adults working with young children. Dr W D Wall in his book, *Child of our Time* describes some of the work of a nursery teacher:

The work of the best Nursery School teachers, from Susan Isaacs onwards, has shown how, by interacting with children at the right moment, by stimulating them to games for which they are ready, but which they would not find out for themselves, by conversation which skilfully enlarges their experience, by arranging of the environment, and in many other ways, the development of children can be accelerated.

The third requirement is the teacher's sensitivity and sound approach to other adults. Unlike most primary and secondary teachers the nursery teacher is never the only adult in her unit. The ratio of adults to children in a nursery environment is 1 :13 (in a nursery school 1 :10) and in a usual group of about 25 children a teacher will work with a nursery nurse. Many separate nursery schools of 40 to 60 children are run as one large unit with all teaching and caring staff working on a team teaching basis. The children are allowed to wander from room to room where different play areas have been laid out – adults are placed in these different areas and work closely together when assessing the developmental play of a child. Clearly a teacher must have a good relationship with her colleagues in order to work in this way.

When dealing with children of three and four years of age the teacher will expect to see and liaise with parents and other friends and relatives on a daily basis. The mere fact that the children are brought into school and undressed by other adults means that the teacher is brought into contact at this level, and she will usually wish to exploit this contact to the full and seize the opportunity to build good school/family relationships. The parental contribution to a nursery will be discussed more fully later, but if the teacher is to have any success with building relationships she must inspire confidence as a person in the parents. A nursery school in particular usually has a varied intake of children from a wide social setting. The teacher will be meeting very different types of parents: they however will see her in a similar light – as the person to whom they are entrusting their very young child, and through whom their child is going to benefit. The initial meeting between parent and teacher is thus of the utmost importance, because if a parent likes what she sees in the teacher she is more likely to feel happy about her child entering the nursery and making his first steps away from the home.

The nursery nurse
The formation of the National Nursery Examination Board in 1945 initiated the two year sandwich course for nursery nurses which is still in existence today. The nursery nurse who passes this course of training has had sound grounding in the development of young children under seven years, and by being aware of the interdependence of these facets of development she is able to cater for their various needs. In former days N.N.E.B. training was strongly biased towards the physical care of the young child – this has now changed and the nursery nurse emerging today has received some training in the importance of developmental play and language development. However, it is clear that the training for a nursery nurse is different from that of a teacher in that it is shorter, more practically orientated and less academic. At the end of their respective courses the two types

of personnel should complement one another in their roles in the nursery.

This partnership cannot be successful if there is strict delineation of role. If the child in the nursery is to receive the full benefit of the two adults working for him there must be areas of close cooperation, joint decisions and a team approach in methodology. The nursery nurse has no more been trained simply to wash paint brushes and clean lavatories, than the teacher has to sit behind a desk all day long. Whilst a team approach is to be recommended, it should be recognized that the teacher is ultimately responsible for the group of children and this very responsibility, together with her particular training means that she must be the policy-maker. The teacher will decide how the unit should operate to provide maximum benefit for each child attending: both the teacher and the nursery nurse will work together to put these aims into practice. Nursery nurses should be allowed full responsibility for planning part of the programme, but this should always be attuned to the overall structure decided by the teacher. There are a number of domestic chores in the nursery which can be shared between the adults. If the nursery environment is to simulate the best in a home situation it will need to reflect the team approach that a family asks of its members. The nursery nurse is recognized as the teacher's assistant, but the true spirit of the partnership comes through in a team teaching approach.

THE NURSERY UNIT AS A TRAINING GROUND

In common with all schools the nursery unit must be prepared to train students in the practical situation. The nursery unit is needed as a training base for teaching and N.N.E.B. students and the maintenance of high standards of training is particularly important at this time when new nursery teaching courses are being established and many more staff are being required to work in new units.

With both types of student, the college and school should make every effort to work closely together. The greater the degree of interaction between the two, the better for the students' morale and greater the chance of any weaknesses in the practical situation coming to light early and being dealt with by the nursery teacher and the college lecturer. The student coming into a nursery is entering a strange environment and however enthusiastic she may be towards her work, however warm her feelings towards young children, she may feel inadequate in the practical group situation. She will be working with adults both older and more experienced than herself who are able to deal with situations more ably and, initially, with greater success than herself. This is not easy, and her confidence may well be shaken until she becomes more familiar with the children and with the nursery routine.

The training of students does throw a responsibility upon the nursery staff. But the wise teacher will recognize that these young girls do have a particular contribution to make to the environment. Young children respond particularly well to young adults. Often a sensitive student who is able to concentrate on one individual or a small group of children, without initially having the anxiety or responsibility of overseeing the entire unit, will be able to develop some very valuable relationships and elicit particular responses in children by virtue of her individual approach.

The nursery nurse student
Some N.N.E.B. students are given a small grant and are trained at a College of Further Education. Others receive a wage from the Local Education Authority during their period of training. The girls usually commence their training at 16 years of age and for part of at least one year they are placed in a nursery unit for two days a week, the remaining three days being spent in their further education at the college. In some areas students will attend college and their practical placements in alternate weeks. Shortened one-year courses have been introduced for mature women over 25 years, and these courses are expanding with the growth of nursery provision.

At one time only nursery schools were considered suitable educational training bases for N.N.E.B. students – with increased nursery expansion this requirement has been waived and nursery nurse students are being placed in nursery classes for at least part of their practical training. Before a nursery unit can be considered as a suitable training base it must be given the opportunity to establish itself, and the staff appointed to the unit will need time in which to relate to the children and build up a stable setting. Formerly any potential nursery training grounds were inspected and passed by an H.M.I. Now increased pressure of work for inspectors and development of more units have caused this to be changed and N.N.E.B. course tutors are now responsible for passing premises; the inspection is often done in cooperation with the Local Authority Nursery or Primary Schools Adviser. The main criteria looked for in a unit are suitable facilities for children of different ages. Is the environment a rich enough one to provide the right example and stimulus for a student in training, and are the staff both willing and capable of coping with the practical work of the student? It should be emphasized that whereas a strong student can be a positive help to a busy member of staff, a weaker individual may well prove to be a burden in the nursery, particularly during the early days of training when she may not be capable of taking on very much responsibility, but must be constantly directed in her work. Nursery staff must be certain that they are ready to tackle the responsibility of a N.N.E.B. student before one is placed with them.

Teachers are understandably anxious to know their responsibilities when agreeing to train a student, and although this is ultimately a matter for individual schools to discuss with course tutors, it might be helpful here to consider what a student will require from her practical training and what will be expected of her by the teacher.

A new student, particularly a sixteen-year-old direct from school, may well have asked for this training without having had any experience of small children. The nursery's first objective must be to give the student plenty of opportunity to mix freely with the children and to learn to relate to them. Sensitivity to the needs of children can only develop gradually, but it is of the utmost importance to the student who is going to succeed in her job. In order to achieve this the student needs to be with a limited number of children in as many different situations as possible, and should be encouraged to observe how these children react in different circumstances and why: the more she gets to know the children, the greater the chance of her establishing some rapport with them.

The student will need to learn about the different materials used in the nursery. She should be given the opportunity to look at these materials from a child's point of view and to experiment with them in order to be sure just what is available for the children to use. Advice should be given on how to present different materials and equipment and information as to *why* they are provided. The student should be aware of how to mix paint and what size brushes are used for small hands. She should learn that certain equipment is used with dry sand and given some idea of the degree of developmental play that can be obtained by using sand as a material in the nursery. All this should of course tie up with her college training in child development. It should become apparent to the student that it is not just sufficient to provide the right materials for the nursery – the staff must ensure that these materials are being used by the children in accordance with their stage of development.

An N.N.E.B. student of 16 years has a very difficult task of almost overnight transformation from being a schoolgirl to being placed on the staff in a school situation. This is not easy for the girl and the third responsibility of the teacher is to ensure that everything is done to ease this change of role. Most students of any calibre will rise to the occasion and accept their new adult status and responsibility – some will take longer than others and will initially be more at ease with the children than their adult colleagues in school. It is important that the nursery teacher and other members of staff accept these young students fully in the staff room and that they are not treated in a condescending manner. If the expectation of the student is high and initial awkwardness is treated with sympathy she is less likely to be inhibited personally, which will restrict her work in the practical situation. Respect for a student does include having respect for her ability to contribute to the work of the nursery. Responsibility must be given, albeit very gradually. When one considers that a first year N.N.E.B. student comes into the practical training ground raw from school, and at the end of that year she must be fully competent with a three to five year age group as an assistant in school (apart from the other careers open to her with young children) it becomes apparent that she must have the fullest possible involvement with the children as soon as she shows herself capable. This is now highlighted with practical training having been cut from three to two days a week. A reasonable first year plan of development for the N.N.E.B. student is set out in Appendix A. If responsibility is slowly increased during the training period to enable the student to participate in all areas of the nursery curriculum, it should be possible for her true potential as a nursery nurse to be realized.

The teacher should enable the student to have the time and opportunity to follow her child observations. These are a requirement of her training course and play an important part in developing her sensitivity to the needs of young children. Often problems are experienced with these initially – the less academic girl will find it difficult to be concise and relevant, and as observation is a skilled art anyway, the student will not be sure what to look for in her child studies. She should be shown how to make the observations objective and later to supplement her findings with her own comments on the child and the situation observed. She should be encouraged to observe and make notes on children at different times of the day and in different activities. As much help as possible in the way of providing necessary background information on the children being studied should be given by the teacher. There is often the very thorny question of confidentiality. However, if students are to be accepted as full members of staff (and preferably so long as they do not live in the neighbourhood of the school) they should be given reasonable access to information on the clear understanding that they are regarded as trustworthy to handle it. Although these child observations are ultimately for presentation to the course tutor at college, the nursery teacher should make it her task to review them and to advise where necessary since, as she knows the children concerned, they are particularly meaningful to her.

Finally the N.N.E.B. student should be given the opportunity to involve herself in every facet of the nursery environment. Clearly she must learn the routine of the domestic tasks involved – as she is on a training course designed for the *care* of the child this aspect will certainly form part of her future job. She must also be trained to see to the simple hygiene and first aid requirements of the children. These two aspects of nursery nursing have always been traditionally part of the course – it is perhaps not so likely that nursery nurses in the past would have been required to meet and talk to parents and other visiting adults in the nursery, to plan displays and projects with the children. All these should be considered part of her job as a nursery nurse today and must be experienced in her training.

The nursery teacher is clearly undertaking to do a great deal if she is to train a nursery nurse student properly. What does she get in return, apart from the considerable satisfaction that she is providing some future nursery unit with a future first class member of staff? Both teacher and children can benefit from a good student. A girl who is reliable and punctual, willing to learn about a new situation and flexible in her response to the many needs of the children will be an asset, and will free the nursery staff at times to deal with particularly difficult children or to talk to parents and other visitors while the students 'hold the fort'. A student should be prepared to receive advice and requests from both the teacher and nursery nurse. The latter can be of particular assistance to her in teaching the daily routine of the nursery.

In summing up we consider that a student should show signs of personal growth during her period of training. In two years she has to develop from a schoolgirl to a fully trained member of the community, capable of coping with a responsible job of work with young children. In order to effect this transformation, the student must be prepared to exploit to the full the facilities and expertise of those in the practical training situation, and to show her worth by making her contribution to the life of the nursery unit.

The teaching student

Whereas nursery nurse students are being trained for many branches of work with young children under seven years, the nursery teacher is responsible specifically to oversee the development of the child of five years and under in the school environment. Until recently there has been a desperate shortage of nursery establishments for training students and the pattern has been for colleges to concentrate on offering students a nursery/infant course covering an age group of three to eight years and for students to gain their practical experience in infant departments. Although it may be recognized as extremely valuable for teachers to be able to follow the full range of development during these early years, the age-span is wide and no form of teacher training can be expected adequately to cover the teaching skills necessary to cope with children from three to eight years. (D Fontana, 'Training of Nursery School Teachers', *Education for Training*, no 93. Spring 1974) Some colleges have already realized this and have started separate Nursery Training courses and this will facilitate specialization in the needs of the younger child.

The teaching student will come to the nursery unit either for block periods of teaching practice or continuously for some part of the week during one or two terms. During this time her responsibilities should be gradually increased enabling her to build up projects with small groups of children and ultimately to take responsibility for the unit. Whereas in other school situations the teacher is able to withdraw from the classroom to allow the final year student complete responsibility for the group, this is not recommended with children of three to four years of age. Constancy of relationship with adults forms an integral part of nursery philosophy and the nursery teacher should ensure that she is available to the children even when the student is running the programme – this should not prove detrimental to the student as it is practical training for working in a team situation. Dealing with adults in the nursery should be one area of special training for the student. Plenty of opportunity should be given for her to mix with parents and to work with the nursery nurse and N.N.E.B. students. Some students who develop their work with the children extremely well may fall down when attempting to develop adult relationships. This situation may be exacerbated when a newly trained teacher is appointed to work with an experienced and mature nursery nurse – clear definition of role and a good team approach are essential for a good working situation.

Again a close relationship between school and college is most important for the student's morale and progress. Occasionally teachers are appointed as tutors by the College of Education. This dual appointment means that the teacher lectures for certain sessions at the college and for the remainder she is in the school situation. Various schemes such as this are being introduced to overcome any gaps between the theory and practice of teaching.

Both college and school need to observe the student carefully to ensure that she is really suited to teaching a nursery age group. A liking of young children is a good start but it is a rather hazy reason for committing oneself to teaching them. However, this is often the only reason that a student may give for opting for this sector of the school community, and quite often she has no experience of dealing with young children, individually or in a group. The student must be made aware of the full implications of nursery teaching – that her future role will be capable of the widest definition and that as a member of a team caring for the young child she will be responsible for his total care. Students training on a nursery/infant course who come for practical training to the nursery after having been in an infant classroom may find initial difficulty in adapting. It is often easier to 'grow' with the child in school practice than the reverse. In this situation the student must be determined to take nothing for granted and not to expect too much of the younger children in behaviour, or competence in skills.

Our nursery units do have a particular responsibility to train nursery teachers to the best of their ability, as it is the quality of these future teachers that will reflect on future nursery provision. It is to be hoped that when students finish their nursery training they will be able to take up scaled posts in nurseries. The lack of nursery schools being built will inevitably mean that any career pattern towards a nursery headship will be limited. This means that nursery teachers must be given a reasonable choice of career development in a primary school, and that service in a nursery unit must be highly regarded and graded accordingly. If this is not clearly recognized there is a danger of nursery teachers becoming 'stuck' in their career – this will doubtless affect the quality of students applying for a nursery training and this in turn can only be reflected by inadequate personnel going into nursery teacher training, advisory and inspectorate posts.

Mature students

Both mature teaching and N.N.E.B. students pose a particular challenge to the teacher in the nursery. It is generally agreed that these older women are highly motivated to be successful during their training and to practise as nursery teachers or nursery nurses directly they have completed the course. This does sometimes mean that they are over-anxious as students. Conversely a younger student who has a rather more relaxed attitude may still be uncertain about her choice of career and teaching students in particular may see their training as a general preparation for different work.

The mature student often has the great advantage of having been a mother herself, and through this is enabled to relate easily to the children – small children in particular will sense the confidence of an older woman. This can also have its dangers, in that a student who has had her own children may be inclined to think that this is enough and that theory is irrelevant. She must learn to realize that being a mother and being a teacher of a group are entirely different, although similar qualities of personality may be required. The discipline of detailed child studies and learning about child development are equally important to the mature student, and she should be encouraged to rethink all previous attitudes and to be self-critical.

Practical difficulties may arise when the older student starts her training. She may initially feel the strain of coping with academic work – essays may prove difficult after so long out of a school situation – and if she has to mix with younger students on the course, the age discrepancy may bring resentments on both sides. As the course progresses the mature student will require a great deal of energy to cope with family demands, practical training and college requirements.

this is an infinitely more stressful situation for her than it will be when she starts full-time work. The teacher must make attempts to understand these problems and to make some allowances. Often an older student can be a valuable addition to the staff, but she may also have special needs.

ADMINISTRATION

The nursery school or unit is dependent for its creation and continued existence on the resources made available to it by the local community through the education authority and it is responsible to the community for the way in which it uses those resources. Apart from providing funds, the local community may, through elected representatives and permanent officials, set down broad policy to be implemented by the school or unit, policy which may at times be at variance with the wishes of teaching staff. Teachers, particularly new teachers, are frequently only vaguely aware of these constraints and their resentment of 'the authorities' might be tempered by a clearer understanding of the situation.

The headteacher

The headteacher is formally responsible to the local education authority and board of managers for the efficient conduct of the school, and informally to the staff to provide satisfactory working arrangements. He or she is in a pivotal position which is not always understood. As an administrator the headteacher can be seen as acting as a 'facilitator', 'mediator' and 'arbiter' (these terms are taken from R G S Brown, *The Administrative Process in Britain*, Methuen, University paperbacks, 1971). As a 'facilitator' the head can be seen as implementing ideas put forward by the authorities or her own staff. If the idea comes from the authorities she will need to 'sell' it to her staff. If the idea comes from her staff, she will need to know how to obtain approval (if it is beyond her authority) and how to obtain finance (if needed). In this role she will need a good knowledge of the machinery of local government, a certain political talent and frequently a fair amount of persistence to deal with red tape. As a 'mediator' the head stands between her staff and the authorities in position of 'broker'. Restraints may be imposed on teachers due to economic difficulties or social conventions. Under these circumstances there are three major possibilities. The head may be able to persuade her staff to keep within the bounds imposed by the authorities. She may attempt to widen the limits within which her staff operate, by finding funds or persuading the authorities to accept teaching innovations. Finally, she may fail to reconcile the staff or obtain concessions from the authorities in which case there will be trouble.

As an 'arbiter' she must choose between priorities. The school will have limited capitation, there will be limits to the concessions she can extract from the authorities; within the school some facilities, e.g. rooms, will be better than others. The head must establish her priorities and this involves judgement on the competing claims of the staff. In the case of a nursery unit attached to a school, this may raise particular problems for the nursery teacher and the head. The nursery teacher may feel, sometimes rightly, that the head does not fully appreciate the weight of the arguments for nursery provision, and the head may feel that the teacher does not understand the difficulties she is working under and the need to look after the other parts of the school. In the end this is really the head's problem to solve.

Internally, to secure the efficient running of the school, the head will need to exercise the functions of management. Firstly, she will need to forecast future eventualities (e.g. decline or increase in the number of children requiring nursery education) and to formulate plans against these eventualities (e.g. expansion or contraction of facilities). She will need to ensure the effective operation of the school, i.e. the provision of materials and staff and the allocation of duties, responsibility and authority to her staff. She will need to exercise command in the sense of giving instructions so that agreed policy is achieved, but in the school setting instructions to fellow professionals will need to be given tactfully if they are to be followed willingly. She will have to exercise control, i.e. checking performance against plans, and taking corrective action, although again in the school context she must not be officious in this duty, nor must she interfere in the professional judgement of her colleagues. Finally amongst the functions of management she should coordinate the actions of her colleagues to achieve the purposes of the school. She will need to motivate her staff, partly by example, partly by showing an interest in them, partly by winning their consent to her policies, and partly by arranging the working conditions of the school so that teachers can obtain self-fulfilment.

The tasks of the headteacher are by no means clearly understood by all headteachers themselves, let alone their staff, but if the school is to serve its community, its children and its staff adequately, the head must discharge her administrative duties properly.

The school secretary
The school secretary may have a crucial role in the administration of the school. She will frequently carry out the bulk of the clerical work; such as returns to the local authority, accounting for the dinner money, the school fund and other cash transactions. Additionally, depending on her experience, she may assist the head in her role as an administrator, particularly if, as so often happens, the school secretary

has an intimate knowledge of the authorities' regulations and an understanding of the workings of local government.

The caretaker

The physical well-being of the school is an essential aspect of its running, and a conscientious caretaker who takes pains over maintenance and cleaning is a boon. In the nursery school the caretaker often represents the only male figure on the premises and may well provide a father figure for the children. A cooperative caretaker may offer to mend toys and do minor repairs in the building. This work is of interest to the children and they should be allowed to watch as a sink is unblocked or a shelf is erected – such observations can lead to the sparking off of interest in various directions (dramatic play, woodwork etc.).

Frequently, and not unnaturally, the objectives of the caretaker may conflict with those of the teaching staff. They will want to make maximum use of facilities, and, especially in the nursery situation, there will be a great deal of messy play. On the other hand the caretaker will want to make sure that everything is clean and in good order – if he did not he would be all the worse at his job. Again this is a problem for the headteacher to resolve in her role of 'arbiter'.

Kitchen staff

Fortunate is the nursery unit where the meals are cooked on the premises and where a full time cook is employed. Many of the older nursery schools have their own kitchens and some units attached to primary schools will have their own facilities. Unfortunately, economies of scale mean that small kitchens are no longer greatly favoured, and container meals from central kitchens are becoming more common.

Where a nursery has its own kitchen the cook may well have a valuable role to play with the children. At her discretion and that of the teacher, children can wander in to see food being prepared and washed. In these days of convenience foods, many young children firmly believe that peas originate from packets and carrots from a tin. If they can see vegetables in the raw state which are then served up for their dinner, gradually realization of their true origins will dawn. Sometimes it is possible to go a stage further and for the nursery to have a kitchen garden where some of the vegetables can be grown and tended by the children – meals can become a great delight if the child realizes that he has helped grow the food he is eating.

A kitchen, by the nature of the domestic routines that take place there, is also a most reassuring spot for a new child who is anxious to find some link with home – five minutes away from the rest of the group watching the cook wash up may soothe a tearful individual where a teacher may not succeed.

The kitchen staff may add a further dimension to the nursery scene. It must not be forgotten, though, that the cook's brief is to prepare and serve meals for the school promptly and in safe and hygienic circumstances – this duty should not conflict with her relationships with the children.

H.M. Inspectors of Education

It is not, of course, just the local authority which has an interest in education, but central government itself. The school's dealings with central government will normally be confined to visits from H.M.I.s, still rather unfairly a source of anxiety to many. This fear of H.M.I.s probably dates back to the days when their role was to ensure that children had achieved a certain standard of education and that government money was being properly spent and when grants could be cut if teachers failed to inculcate a minimum standard of literacy and numeracy. Naturally, no teacher would welcome unfavourable criticism from an H.M.I., but they have moved on from their strict nineteenth century role of inspection, and now provide support to teaching staff by spreading sound practices over as wide a field as possible and by assisting teachers in their work. Indeed, since 1968 regular formal inspections have been abandoned altogether. Additionally, their reports may assist in obtaining better resources for schools because, other things being equal, no education authority will want adverse reports, however confidential, on its provision sent to the Department of Education and Science.

Advisers

At a local level, support is given to teachers and headteachers by advisers, who have their own channels of communication with the education authority and who may be able to draw on their knowledge of practice in other schools to give advice. Advisers are often particularly involved with probationary teachers, providing reassurance and advice during the first year of teaching.

To sum up, schools cannot and should not act in a vacuum. Administrative machinery must exist between schools and sponsoring authorities, and it must exist internally to ensure the smooth functioning of the school.

3

The nursery and the community

THE COMMUNITY NURSERY UNIT

This final chapter of part I, although inevitably linked with the two
previous chapters, is probably the most important. Having planned
the building and materials in the nursery unit and analysed the role
of the adults employed to work there, what type of environment is to
be provided for these small children? How can the effects of nursery
provision be most beneficially felt, thus justifying the amount of
money that is to be involved in the project? I suggest that the answers
to these questions lie in seeing what factors favourably affect the
child during his earliest years of life and to concentrate on
strengthening, building and extending these. If we look at
A H Halsey's statement that 'a half-time pre-school programme lasting
for one year has only taken up 2% of the child's waking life before he
enters full-time school,' we realize that even the most ambitious of
nursery schemes has little chance of making an impact when working
in isolation from the other aspects of the child's upbringing. The first
three years of a child's life are usually spent in a home which is
situated in a particular social setting. The quality of the child's
parents, the type of home and the accompanying social scene
determine the life style of that child during his early years. During the
third or fourth year a part or full-time nursery place may become
available for the child and he will start his formal education. The
teacher must realize that she is not dealing with new material but a
product of three years past experience, and this is the child's starting
point at school.

It may be that he has been fortunate and these years have been in
a loving, stable home with plenty of stimulus on which to feed his
development. In this case the nursery will wish to reinforce this
environment and merely add to it by providing social opportunities in
a group situation, and the services of a professionally trained person
to extend the child further. At the other extreme is the child from a
broken home, in material need and with little stability or animation in
his life. In this instance the teacher must seek to enrich the child's
environment, adding the dimension of school in a way which he will

understand and to which he will want to respond. In both these cases, as the nursery unit provides the beginnings of the school system, the term 'pre-school' can be a misleading one. If we regard it as 'pre-infant school' there is a danger that this descriptive term will be the sum total of the nurseries' aims. Inevitably each stage of development prepares the way for the next, and in this way the child of three is gradually prepared to enter the infant school environment where he will, among many other things, acquire the more formal skills of reading and writing. He is also being prepared for a much greater task – that of maturation and emerging as a fully independent adult in the community. This process began with birth and can only terminate in death. His formal education will only be an interlude in this span of time. It is also only going to be of use if it is made relevant to the world in which the child is already living and in particular to his immediate community setting.

The other reason for establishing a school with good community relations is to encourage parents to become involved and interested in their children's education, and this will be easier if the school is regarded as an open rather than a closed unit. Research for the Plowden report showed that home background, particularly parental attitudes, was more important than the school when assessing what affected a child's performance. The Coleman report in 1966 was the result of a survey sponsored by the United States Office of Economic Opportunity, designed mainly to see what differences there were in school facilities for black and white children, and whether any such differences affected the ability to learn. The report showed, rather unexpectedly, that the school facilities for black and white children did not vary greatly, and that the lower performance of the black group was largely due to inferior home background. (This report was subsequently criticized for its use of verbal ability tests which do not do justice to the more disadvantaged child.) J W B Douglas in *Home and School* states that 'a child's ability to do well in his work at school is to a certain degree dependent on the encouragement he gets from his parents, the sort of home he has and the academic record of his school.' These findings point to the great importance of the child's environment out of school, and they apply to every child, regardless of his background.

Let us consider particularly the certain group of children who are radically affected in a negative way by this discovery. These children are the product of the 'cycle of deprivation', in which certain social problems recur consistently through generations. The term 'deprivation' can be used to describe any circumstances which may prevent a person from reaching his potential. The deprivation may be physical, emotional or intellectual and the causes may be genetic, economic or social. It will manifest itself at all levels of society – the neglected middle-class child of professional parents may be considered deprived and most children from broken homes suffer some form of deprivation although they may be financially secure. Dr Kellmer Pringle writing in *The Needs of Children* lists five groups of children considered disadvantaged or 'at risk'. These are children with physical or mental handicaps, those in one-parent families, children who have to live apart from their parents for longer or shorter periods, those belonging to minority groups, and children in large families with low incomes. The most vulnerable group is probably this last one at the foot of the social and economic scale and it is this socially deprived group that we will consider as the one most deserving of our scarce resources.

The longitudinal study of the National Child Development Bureau describes different social classes by classifying their occupations. Using this system of classification, groups four and five are the semi-skilled and unskilled manual group of workers. These are the main sector of the population that will hold the children considered 'at risk'. Although it must be remembered that perfectly stable homes may exist within this sector, the large majority of social group five will live in Educational Priority Areas. Typically these areas will have a high number of family breakups, poor housing and overcrowding, high unemployment, larger families and a low school performance from the children.

The White Paper in 1973 recognized that every child should have the right to some form of pre-schooling and that within the next ten years nursery education should become available without charge, within the limits of the demand estimated by Plowden, to those children of three and four whose parents wish them to benefit from it. The White Paper also recognized that this nursery expansion would take time and that during the initial stages some priorities for provision should be established: '. . . priority will be given during the early stages of the programme to areas of disadvantage.' As a result of Plowden asking in 1966 for 'positive discrimination in favour of schools in areas of high social need', the E.P.A. project was established by Dr Halsey in 1968. The objectives of this project were to increase the involvement of parents in their children's education and to increase the sense of community responsibility. The importance of pre-school provision was once again reaffirmed. Children of five years from E.P.A.s were found to score well below average in any vocabulary tests. Clearly anything that was to be done to stem deprivation must start at the earliest possible age. The school which recognizes that the child cannot be helped in isolation will direct its efforts towards helping maintain a support system in the community for families beset by multiple problems.

The moment of entry to nursery or infant school is a traumatic one for many children, but socially disadvantaged children enter with inherent difficulties as they grapple not only with an unfamiliar world, but one that is in complete contrast to their home. The value which has been placed upon education (particularly the learning that takes place in school) is a middle-class concept. Parents from social groups four and five are unable to plan their lives efficiently from week to week and most have little control over their economic status – they are certainly unable to grasp the importance of planning for a future for their children. This group sees little reason for encouraging their children at school, although as we will see later, if approached in the right manner they can prove to be cooperative parents.

The gulf in attitudes extends into the field of language. Bernstein studied the use of language by different social groups and put forward the hypothesis that the working-class use only a restricted code of conversation and the middle-class use both the restricted and the elaborated code. The former relies mainly on the present tense and is mainly descriptive: the latter tends to be more analytical, is wider in range and can invoke the powers of logical argument. Bernstein's findings are very relevant to the child entering the nursery for the first time. As Dr Joan Tough says, 'the relationship with adults which disadvantaged children have learnt to expect is one that does not foster the explorative uses of language'. (1974) This in turn is not conducive to a learning situation and is one more hindrance for the socially deprived child to overcome. It is seen in a most intensive form in the immigrant child, particularly those newly arrived in this country in whom language deficiency is accompanied by culture shock. Some of these immigrant children have been wrongly labelled educationally subnormal in the past because of their apathy and inability to adapt to so alien a learning situation. Their need for special help remains.

The I.L.E.A. have recently published their research results after two years during which they poured £300,000 worth of aid into E.P.A. schools, including various community projects and fostering of home-school links. Rather depressingly the progress made by these children after such aid was only marginal in both behaviour and academic attainment. However the results are more significant when it is seen that the control group of children who did not receive the aid, not only did not improve in attainment, but steadily deteriorated. This reinforces Douglas' findings in *Home and School*.

If we accept Dr Kellmer Pringle's premise (1974) that the child's environmental background is most influential during the early years of life it is clearly necessary to attempt to combat social deprivation during the period of nursery schooling, and in some cases even earlier. Results from the I.L.E.A. projects indicate that community school schemes can help to stem the problem of deprivation, but as yet it is too big an assumption to say that they are a solution for social ills. It is worthwhile noting Bernstein's comment that 'schools cannot compensate for society.' Unless social reform is sufficiently thorough to eliminate poverty, whatever the school may seek to do in the community will only partially succeed.

We must now look to see how a community school, and particularly one catering for pre-school needs will operate. As described by Eric Midwinter the community school '. . . ventures out into the community. The community school welcomes in the community. Ideally all barriers would collapse completely and the borders become indistinguishably blurred.' This is possibly a somewhat extreme and altruistic view in areas where school is regarded with utmost suspicion and teacher-parent relationship is one of 'them and us'. However when we consider the early nursery institutes introduced by Rachel and Margaret McMillan we can see that their aims were community orientated if somewhat paternalistic. All early nursery superintendents visited the children and parents in their home setting, and mother's clubs were formed for the mothers of the children in the nursery. These clubs usually met once a week and were primarily intended as social occasions to provide some therapy and relief for adults who were heavily burdened with poverty and social misery. Likewise early nursery projects in Scotland often invoked voluntary help for daily organization. In 1935 the first nursery school in Fife was opened as the result of a public meeting where the project was explained and voluntary helpers and gifts of money were requested. Unemployed men offered to adapt and repair furniture to make it suitable for young children. (*Before Five*, 1971)

These ventures were a far cry from the isolated institutions that many schools became in subsequent years. However, early tradition did make its mark on the nursery sector. Patrick McGeeney (1972) quotes examples of three nursery schools he visited where the fullest possible parental co-operation was sought and obtained. It is to be hoped that the practice of these schools will rub off onto the heads of primary schools where nursery units are being built.

Schools in general have come a long way towards involving themselves in the neighbourhood. Notices formerly found in school playgrounds stating that no parent is allowed on the premises are now disappearing and more head teachers are expressly inviting parents and visitors to see the school and to add their contribution to it. The first step in establishing a nursery unit which is orientated towards the neighbourhood is to make it physically accessible to the people who are going to use it. Plowden advised that any new nursery schools should be built on housing estates and near blocks of flats. Unless nursery provision, which is voluntary (and often part-time) is placed in the areas it is designed to serve, there will always be a nucleus of mothers who are not prepared to make the journey to and from school.

A community establishment should include a successful information service. The Newcastle Action Group, reporting on *Working-Class Mothers and Pre-School Education*, said 'it is not reasonable to expect parents, and especially those in areas of high social deprivation to know intuitively about nursery education provisions and how to set about making an application.' Today, even with the focus of attention on the importance of pre-school education, some parents from all sectors of society are uninformed or misinformed about what provision is desirable for their young children and how they can obtain it. Similarly, working-class parents are shown by Jackson and Marsden (1962) to have little idea of what to expect when their child enters primary school. These parents must be made cognisant of what is available and also of their own vital role in their child's stages of development. Contrary to popular opinion about disadvantaged parents being uninterested in the educational needs of their children various research (Chazan, Laing and Jackson, 1971) has pointed to this not being so. The unresponsiveness of these parents has been to the traditional 'middle-class' approach. Newsletters, notices and lectures usually fall on barren ground with parents from priority areas and, as we will discuss later, a more personal approach tends to be more successful.

Apart from the functions outlined in the section on administration, the head of a school should be aware that a large part of her job is in public relations. In the case of the nursery unit, the more people who know about what facilities exist for young children the more interest is likely to be stimulated and in turn the more opportunities should be provided for learning situations. Pre-school displays in public places, showing examples of unaided children's work, literature about and for young children and photographs of them at play should be regular features in a neighbourhood. Nursery open days, giving opportunity for the public to see buildings and equipment and to talk with staff over refreshments should be offered to all.

Part of the E.P.A. project in the West Riding was to establish a market stall which acted as an information and advice centre and stocked a range of children's books and toys which were not available locally. Schools generally co-operated with the scheme and informed parents about the stall. Mothers of young children were particularly anxious to buy toys, and many of the public came to the stall for information about education in general. There was also a supply of welfare forms and advice on how to apply for free meals and social security. This scheme was essentially practical – supplying goods and counselling where they were needed – and the response from the public suggested that the market stall is a way of opening education into the community.

The aim of this type of publicity is to 'demystify' the process of education of very young children and to state clearly to as wide a section of the public as possible that early investment in children's development reaps dividends. This can not be done in a school that is only interested in teachers and children. The child must be seen in his social setting and his education tackled from there.

LINKS WITH OTHER STATUTORY BODIES

When looking at what is needed for the optimum growth of young children it becomes apparent that these needs are interdependent – from birth a baby's development depends upon the satisfactory meeting of physical, emotional and intellectual needs. This is true throughout childhood. The nursery teacher who sees her role as attending to the overall needs of the child will realize that little can be done to stimulate developmental play if medical attention is required or if home conditions are unsatisfactory. The teacher, whilst regarding herself as the overseer to the child's growth must realize her limitations and recognize that in certain medical and social matters specialized help must be sought. A teacher can only be alert to the needs of each individual in her particular group – if she is going to attempt to diagnose and deal with needs which are outside the scope of her knowledge and experience she is likely to do more harm than good. The teacher must however know how and where she can obtain the necessary help.

Plowden recommended that nursery schools or units should be situated near to or with other facilities for young children. Where this is not so, lack of liaison can prove to be a real danger. For instance, health visitors may refer a child to a nursery unit because of physical or emotional need, and once she is given a place at school any further contact may cease, simply because of the pressure of a heavy case load or the difficulties of visiting. Or a child may well be referred to a consultant at the hospital, and no copy of any medical report is sent to the head teacher. Duplication of duty is a further likelihood – a family in social difficulty with young children can be inundated with visitors: educational welfare officer, health visitor, social security officer, teacher and social worker could all be concerned with the same case and feel that it was in their province to visit and advise. This duplication is a total waste of resources and can only cause confusion in a family where pressures are already high. By providing these various welfare agencies on the same site as the school these dangers are not necessarily averted, but it does become more practicable to work together. Kellmer Pringle (1974) says that 'in order to promote greater interdisciplinary co-operation of the 'grass-roots', people need to come together from different professional fields, and from statutory and voluntary services in a variety of activities based on the school as a neighbourhood resource centre.'

The second reason for easy access or dual use of school buildings is surely for the convenience of the family. The mother with several young children and no spare money for buses can spend an enormous amount of her time and energy travelling to and from the doctor's surgery seeing to all the necessary pre-school immunisations and having dental checkups for her children, quite apart from checking on all the other childhood ailments. The National Child Development Study showed that families from social class groups four and five used medical and dental services noticeably less than other families. There is no clear reason why this is so, but one possible answer is the lack of accessibility and confusion in the parent's mind as to which agency is responsible for what aspect of the child. Surely if medical, social counselling and educational facilities were grouped on one campus, or in the case of a community centre under one roof, the parent would be more inclined to use these facilities. So often a doctor's or dentist's surgery is not geared to the needs of young children – a pre-school centre with the four-year-old in the nursery unit and the baby having a medical checkup next door is infinitely more helpful and practical from the mother's point of view. In Brenda Crowe's words: 'Anything that improves the mother's health and happiness has a profound effect upon her husband and children.' (Crowe, 1973)

One area where some measure of interdepartmental co-operation is being sought is in extended day care provision. Although the White Paper recommended that 15% of future nursery provision should be for a full day, suggesting that this would meet particular social needs, in fact a nursery day from 9 to 3.30 does little to provide a satisfactory solution for our most needy children. Where the social need is greatest, both parents will probably be working full-time (possibly on a shift system with one parent at home during the day to sleep).

Most pre-school children of working parents are cared for by full-time childminders. In some areas the childminders have long waiting lists and are certainly not prepared to be employed part-time to bring and collect children from the nursery and only mind them for a few hours in their home. There is every possibility of a part-time or even a full-time place in a nursery unit being refused by a working parent because of the problems of unrealistic hours. (See *Education* vol 142, pp 3–14, 26 October 1973). In this case only further extended hours will provide a satisfactory answer for the family. Where a few day nurseries have made this provision for children from nought to five years in the past, there is now an experimental movement towards the Nursery Centre which is open from 7.30 am to 6 pm for approximately fifty weeks of the year. Such a centre is a product of interdepartmental co-operation between the Social Services and the Education Department and the aim is to achieve a measure of dual provision for the child. This project involves a nursery unit and a day nursery sharing the same facilities and the same building. Children can attend for just school hours, or, if their need is warranted, can be accepted in the day nursery for the full day. Part of that day will be spent in the nursery class working with nursery teachers. The extreme ends of the day will be organized by nursery nurses as these are considered to be the times of day when a child requires more 'caring' attention than educational provision.

The success of such ventures is clearly dependent on the amount of interdepartmental cooperation and on satisfactory staffing. Instances where the nursery and day nursery have shared the same building, but have existed as two separate entities render the scheme an absurdity. Some staff are reluctant to work on a shift basis and this is necessary to keep the centre open for a practical number of hours and during school holidays. However, if these difficulties are overcome, the projects may well lead to a new dimension of provision for young children with the various departments supporting one another.

There are now six such Nursery Centres in the country, with several more in various stages of planning. One of the common problems when it comes to interdepartmental working is the decision as to who is ultimately in charge. Is it the Nursery Matron financed by the Social Services, or the headteacher from the Education Department? Ultimately there must be only one head – where centres have been running with two people ultimately responsible, inevitable conflicts have arisen. Ideally, the person appointed needs to be a trained nursery teacher with some medical or social work background or qualification – perhaps this type of training should be made available in Colleges of Education (see the section on Home Visitors).

These projects are still at an experimental stage and time will tell how successful and truly integrated a scheme they are. They are providing an exciting means of seeing how the educational and social services can work together for the same child, but they also entail expensive, purpose built establishments, and even if the present projects are successful, widespread expansion is unlikely in the near future.

Whether buildings are situated together or not there is every reason for all professional workers dealing with young children to liaise closely. Some of the workers involved are described below.

Doctors, health visitors and social workers must all come into contact at some stage with families where they would wish to refer the young child for a place in a nursery unit. This may be because of behavioural problems on the part of the child, because of tension in the home, mental illness on the part of the mother, or general lack of home stimulus and consequent poor language development – to name but a few difficulties. Often, children who are referred by workers to the nursery have poor environmental background and it is this type of family that needs the fullest support from all social, educational and medical agencies.

Health visitors are perhaps the obvious people to consider when it comes to the needs of the baby and pre-school child at home. Although originally the health visitor's task was to see to the health and hygiene of the family, now her role is greatly extended and most good health visitors view the young child in his total environment and will attempt to remedy any serious deficiency in the home. Because the health visitor sees the mother and baby from the earliest age and can develop a close relationship with the family, she is often the obvious person to recommend when and where a child should apply for a nursery place. A liaison health visitor should be attached to the nursery unit, and regular meetings should take place between her and the headteacher. Specific applications for urgent nursery places can then be considered quickly and where necessary the appointed health visitor can check on any routine medical questions in the nursery and provide background information on specific families that may be needed.

Health visitors may also prove to be a valuable link between the teacher and school doctor, G.P. or paediatrician where children are having medical attention. She may accompany the school doctor when he does medical inspections of the children in the nursery. All children should have a medical before entering a nursery unit and further inspections should take place during the time in the nursery. This is most useful for screening the child for any defects that may be remedied before starting primary school. It cannot be stressed too strongly that when a child is referred for a nursery place and is admitted, the headteacher should always receive a copy of the medical case history. From then on the school is going to be the one agency most closely concerned with the child on a daily basis, apart from his family – if full medical facts are not divulged the nursery is often unable to assess the child's development properly and much of the value of the placement may be lost. In certain cases, copies of all the child's medical appointments should be sent to the unit in order to ensure that these appointments are kept.

Educational Welfare Officers can be of assistance in seeing that nursery places are fully utilized. Sadly many of the areas most in need of pre-school provision are the ones where parents are too apathetic or overburdened to bring them regularly. This is especially frequent where the provision is only part-time. A careful watch has to be kept on this as, although priority of placement must be given to these children, nursery places are scarce and no waste of places can be tolerated. The Educational Welfare Officer will visit these families to see if the place is really necessary for the child. It should be emphasized that in defining the role of health visitor and welfare officer as home visitors, the value of the headteacher or nursery teacher visiting homes is not to be underrated. This is a particular facet of home/school relations that we will be explaining, and the need to ensure application to a nursery unit or to guard against persistent non-attendance are but two aspects of this relationship.

Social workers often become involved with young children and their families at the point of breakdown and where there is a danger of the children being taken into care. Occasionally the offer of a nursery place may be sufficient to relieve the mother of some of the tensions of coping with an active pre-schooler when she is already overburdened with marital and household problems. Clearly when an offer of such a place can prevent the child from being taken away from the family, it should be regarded as topmost priority. Having placed the child in the nursery the social worker and school should be in regular contact to assess what benefits are accruing to the child from his school environment and how the family situation is improving. If the situation worsens, the child should be watched closely for any signs of child battering or physical neglect at home which may point to the need for greater family support. There may be a place for informal meetings of the headteacher (or nursery teacher if relieved from her group), social worker and parent over a cup of coffee. If the parent can be made aware that these two adults are a team prepared to help her and her family without any stringent pressures attached, barriers may be broken down and help may be asked for before the situation becomes irretrievable.

If any nursery or infant department is asked to define the most common problem found among young children today, many will say minor speech problems. There are a variety of opinions as to why so many young children seem unable to speak distinctly or express themselves linguistically, but the main reasons seem to be the preponderance of television, the lack of understanding on the part of parents that it is essential to speak to their young babies and consequently evoke an imitative response, and the lack of time that adults are prepared to spend with their children. This problem is a very real one and with a nursery ratio of about one adult to thirteen children, the nursery teacher and her assistant do not have the time to spend on regular individual speech sessions with a number of children, nor have they the expertise to cope with the varying degrees of linguistic handicap. This is the field of the speech therapist and every nursery unit does need to have regular visits from such specialists who can preferably work with small groups of children or individuals in a quiet area or small room adjacent to the nursery. If this is a regular occurrence and takes place on nursery premises, the child is caused the least possible amount of disruption. No child will respond so well if he has to attend a special clinic for this purpose; in unfamiliar surroundings the child feels that he is different and this can give rise to further inhibition. If the speech therapist can work on the nursery premises and can advise the nursery teacher how to follow up her specialist sessions with the child the speech problem can be tackled without undue anxiety on the part of the parent or child.

This, then, is the ideal situation — however in practice the situation is far from ideal at the moment. In 1972 there were said to be just under 1000 practising speech therapists in the country. According to Professor Court, formerly Professor of Child Health at Newcastle, these were 'unevenly distributed, often single-handed and generally isolated from paediatricians both in hospital and in pre-school and school health service and from psychologists, child psychiatrists and teachers.'

The situation is no different today and it means that only the most severe speech handicaps are referred to a therapist and these may be seen after a considerable waiting period. Most dangerous is the tendency to deal with speech difficulties only when the child reaches primary school age. Because the speech therapist is so overworked she may tend to give priority to older children and may be over-reassuring to parents about younger children's difficulties being due to general immaturity which will right itself. In fact, of course, it is essential to deal with linguistic problems at the pre-school stage where the staff-child ratio is more generous, before the child becomes too self-conscious about his difficulty and before he is faced with accompanying problems in his acquisition of more formal skills such as reading. The only answer to this lack of specialists is greater recognition of the speech therapist and consequently better status and pay conditions for a field of work which requires a long period of training.

Apart from language difficulties, the nursery is the ideal environment to note any particular weaknesses. Deficiencies of sight and hearing which may not have been apparent to the parent may be suspected by the teacher and arrangements made for suitable tests. Lack of co-ordination, inability to socialize, and slow response to situations generally are examples of danger signals in children. The teacher will not be able to diagnose the problem in every case, this is not her role, but she should be alert to any deficiency in normal development and able to bring in the specialist as the need arises. It is necessary to stress again that any assessment of the child should as far as possible take place in the home or the school. A psychologist's office, or a doctor's consulting room is alien territory to the child and can only place him at a disadvantage.

The majority of small children do not visit a dentist until they have toothache – by which time the tooth is often beyond redemption. Lack of knowledge about suitable diet and dental hygiene among families means that children from these families have no chance to develop healthy first teeth and consequently this affects the permanent second teeth. Preventive dentistry is essential to stop this vicious circle. Unfortunately the lack of school dentists in some parts of the country is almost as severe as the lack of speech therapists, and this means major problems in achieving an effective service for families to help them prevent decaying teeth, as well as dealing with the effects of decay. The early years of life – from conception onwards – are crucial for sound dental development and regular visits from the dentist should be part of every nursery routine. Dental problems are likely to affect all levels of society, but as with other weaknesses they will probably be more prominent in social groups four and five where mothers are not aware of the effects of the neglect of teeth cleaning and a large diet of sweets. These same mothers probably had an inadequate diet themselves in pregnancy and a lack of calcium could well have resulted in poor enamel formation in their children. A sensible diet at school without sweets, and regular dental checkups will help these children to some degree, but the burden of seeing to their healthy dental development will rest in the home and a lot of information and advice about the care of teeth needs to be given to parents.

We have outlined some of the agencies which are involved with some part of the child. All these needs must be attended to and as they are dealt with the different individuals concerned can all add some extra dimension to the child's case history : is he physically fit, functioning at a normal level, suffering from stress within the family or has some minimal handicap been diagnosed ? All this information is essential to the nursery teacher who must know where she is starting with the child before she can chart his development. Clearly then these agencies need to work closely together and to work with the teacher. The most effective relationship will be one of good regular liaison, rather than contact only in time of emergency. Each worker needs to know about any new developments affecting the young child even if these are not directly within his field. Nursery units should inform all other personnel if there is any change in their admission policies – health visitors and social workers should continue to feed in information about families of young children who are in the nursery. The stability of this relationship should mean that there is a constant awareness of the contributions and limitations of the other side, that there is constant interchange of ideas and that this leads to greater flexibility by all concerned.

LIAISON WITH VOLUNTARY BODIES WHO HAVE PRE-SCHOOL PROVISION

In preparing for the expansion of Nursery Education, Local Authorities will need to take account of the other facilities for under-fives, existing or planned, so as to prepare a scheme for their areas in which nursery classes and schools, voluntary playgroups, day nurseries and other forms of day care all play their part. The Government attach importance to a *full assessment of local resources* and will welcome diversity in provision so long as it is efficient and there is no sacrifice of standards in the education and care of children . . . consultation with voluntary bodies will also be necessary in many areas.
(*Education: a framework for expansion*, p 6)

We have already stressed that in order to provide a comprehensive and relevant service to families with young children there must be a united front amongst different departments. This applies equally to our relationship with non-statutory bodies, and there appear to be three main reasons for liaising with these organizations who are themselves concerned with young children.

Any such group will have opportunities to establish informal links with families, and are in a position to refer particular children for a nursery school place. A voluntary worker may well be accepted in a household where a teacher or social worker who has a more defined 'label' will be regarded with suspicion. Clearly there is a time when voluntary help is not enough for the child who has severe behaviour problems or whose language is limited. Voluntary recommendations to nursery units are a further way of making state nursery provision accessible to the most needy group of children.

We must also acknowledge the findings from the Halsey Report that the most effective form of fighting deprivation in young children and providing for them educationally is to set up varying pre-school projects, both statutory and voluntary according to the needs of the local community, and this is echoed in the above paragraph from the White Paper. We should accept that a nursery school or attached nursery unit is by no means the only or best way of providing early education for all young children. Widely scattered rural areas need to have special consideration here: a nursery class attached to the village school with young children being 'bussed' in from surrounding areas is not a reasonable answer for this type of community. There are problems of who accompanies the children on the school bus, what happens if the child is ill whilst at school and the rural home has no telephone or transport, how does one provide half-time provision for children living a good distance from the school? (In some areas this has meant two or three full days a week in the nursery. Full day provision must be provided for some children, but surely we do not want to propose it when the only need is an administrative one?)

Young children in hospital, gypsy children and children in homeless family units are minority groups who will not benefit from a traditional nursery programme. Imaginative use of statutory and voluntary bodies is needed to serve these children who are already suffering from certain disadvantages, and should not be penalized further.

Thirdly if a child is referred by a voluntary worker and accepted into a nursery, the worker will be of great value in providing background information on the child and his family. This provides yet another link in the team who should work and liaise together to support the family that is not coping in the community.

The contribution of playgroups to the community

The Playgroup movement is the most significant development for young children during the past twenty years. The Save the Children Fund started semi-voluntary groups in 1954 staffed by nursery nurses with mothers as extra members of the staff. The Pre-School Playgroups Association, now the main representative body for playgroups, started groups in 1960 after a petition to Parliament for more nursery provision had failed. Playgroups are many and various – some staffed by trained people, some run by mothers. Premises may be in church halls or private homes, some even have their own premises which they have built themselves with the aid of a grant or loan from the local council.

Standards of groups also vary greatly, some providing little more than a childminding service for small children, and some aspiring to make provision to the best standard that any nursery unit can offer. The P.P.A. does not lay down any strict policy on standards, although guidelines and advice are available: it is up to the Department of Health and Social Services to see that premises are inspected.

Given this wide variation in playgroup provision there is one type of group which offers more than others – this is the community run playgroup, devised and run by parents for their own children. This type of playgroup has reflected a strong wish for many parents that they want to be included and have some say in the education of their children. Dr W D Wall, Dean of the Institute of Education at the University of London, says that 'if we accept that the quality of parental care is the most important factor in a child's development, certainly in his earliest years, then one of our chief concerns should be to support and encourage mothers in their demanding, vital role.'

This support and encouragement for the parents to be a self-help group is the chief contribution that playgroups have made to pre-schooling. Although early nursery schools did have a form of parent participation it must be admitted that it was a paternalistic type – the experts bestowing information on the ignorant. I hope we have now learnt that, as Lady Plowden says,

. . . there must in all classes be absolute equality between those who, though professionally trained, have only limited responsibility, and the parents, who whatever their education, or lack of it, have the ultimate responsibility for their children. Because playgroups start from the grassroots, and are often run by people who have no professional training, there can be no possible rift between those who know and those who don't. (*Education*, 14 July 1972, p 72)

The playgroups' second great asset is the degree of enthusiasm and initiative of a body of people who have not waited for the state to provide for the under-fives, but have developed something themselves. The energy and spontaneity of such a movement is apparent when one looks at the tremendous growth and strength of the playgroup movement over the years. This pressure group has been most articulate in making known the needs of young children.

The third contribution of the movement springs from its possible handicap. Playgroups are voluntary organizations and although they are now assisted by central and local grants from social services and education authorities, each playgroup is self-supporting and has to charge fees to cover the cost of rent, heating and equipment. This does mean that often groups are run on a shoestring, but their poverty of circumstances has meant that in many groups tremendous ingenuity and creativity has been used in making equipment and providing activities for the children. Often when a nursery would look to a catalogue to order materials, a playgroup has been forced to improvise and this improvsiation has led to further open-ended channels of play.

Finally as a dynamic community venture, playgroups are able to provide for children's varying needs. Clearly groups first originated in more aware middle-class areas where articulate parents organized action, but they have spread to many deprived, urban areas where mothers are also involved and helping to run groups. The quasi-voluntary groups run by the Save the Children Fund provide facilities for the minority groups of children such as the homeless and those in hospital, and Halsey recommended that Playmobiles might be used to visit rural areas or high rise flats where there was no facility for playgroup or nursery premises. These playmobiles would probably be staffed by a teacher and voluntary assistance would be obtained from the mothers on a rota basis.

These then are the main advantages of playgroups When looking at their disadvantages as compared to nursery units, the main difficulties appear to be the lack of any national training, of an established standard for playgroups, and of purpose built premises.

While the majority of playgroup supervisors attend some locally organized course run by the P.P.A., the Local Authority or by the Workers' Educational Association, these courses differ in length, in content, and in standard. Often the authorities find difficulty in employing suitable tutors for the courses, and although students undoubtedly benefit from the subject matter (as expressed by their general enthusiasm on any such course) there is no means of knowing how much has been absorbed as the courses have no assessment or examination at the end.

When mentioning the advantages offered by playgroups, these are, in the main, only offered by the community based group. It must be emphasized that no two playgroups are alike. They may be run as a business, or as a non-profit making body, or as a charity. They may only offer a dubious social benefit to a few children by bringing them together in the supervisor's home for rather limited play activities, or they might be run by people who have attended good playgroup courses and are aiming in their provision to further the all round development of the child and his mother. This great range of standards is a drawback for public relations – good playgroups are sometimes equated with poor ones and there is often internal confusion as to what playground aims are. The P.P.A. does provide guidelines here, but there are still many playgroups which are not affiliated to this association.

Those playgroups operating in church halls and similar accommodation with no real permanence, inadequate storage facilities and lack of outside space are labouring under very real difficulties. Where there is no opportunity to display paintings, or set up a nature table which can be left, or leave a half-finished brick construction so that the children can continue work the following day, the atmosphere and standard of play offered must suffer. The setting up and putting away of every piece of equipment daily also imposes extra strains on the playgroup staff.

There can be no doubt of the great value of the playgroup movement, and also no question of its importance diminishing in the near future whilst nursery provision is developing at such a slow rate. Nursery units have both something to learn from playgroups and something to offer in the way of support. The way to the most satisfactory development of both bodies lies through close liaison.

How can we achieve this liaison? Firstly, I believe, through regular visiting by the nursery teacher or head to the local playgroups, and of playgroup personnel to the nursery. Familiarity with one another's routine is an important start to common discussion. Playgroups with their roots in the community are aiming primarily at the involvement and growth of the parent along with her child and for the development of a more responsible attitude towards child rearing. Nursery units with specialists on their staff are aiming more for a higher developmental standard of play for children and again for some form of parental involvement, if only because that child belongs to these parents. These aims differ only in emphasis: there is at present room for both lines of thought and work, and to be well acquainted with each other's work is the first step to close co-operation.

The headteacher or nursery teacher could be invited on to the playgroup committee — any community group will wish to have a committee representing the needs of the locality, and a teacher is a good person to have as an expert on young children. (It must, however, be remembered that teachers are not always aware of the limitations and possibilities of playgroup work in a hall or house.)

Training courses for playgroup personnel are very important indeed. Marianne Parry and Hilda Archer found that the best playgroup workers were those who had attended some course, preferably one lasting for two or three years. Most areas offer some form of basic playgroup course lasting for eight to ten weeks and which is essentially practical in content, allowing all present to become familiar with different materials used in playgroups. A longer or 'second level' course is then sometimes organized where students (mothers) can examine material and concepts in greater depth and be given some training in child development. Surely these courses should take place in the nursery unit where all the requisite practice facilities are on hand, and the atmosphere is right for the course material. The nursery teacher will also provide a useful tutor for some aspects of the course, so long as she has built up some familiarity with playgroups and can relate her theories and practice to their needs.

Brenda Crowe (1973) suggests that future planning projects should ensure that a nursery school aims to support and advise several playgroups within its perimeter. 'Provision should be made for suitable halls to accommodate playgroups, sited round the central pivot of each nursery school. This would enable each playgroup to have its own inspiration point within easy access, both for observation and advice.'

Hillfields Nursery Centre in Coventry, in conjunction with the Community Education project, has established a slightly adapted form of this recommendation. Since 1973 annexes have been started in the nursery centre area. Each of these annexes has been developed and is being run by a trained teacher, responsible to the head of the nursery centre, but her supporting staff are mothers. This appears to be an ideal form of liaison between different bodies to serve local needs.

Finally there should be much closer working between such bodies as the Save the Children Fund, the Women's Royal Voluntary Service, the Pre-School Playgroups Association and the British Association for Early Childhood Education (for a full list of these bodies see appendix E) at the national level. Some attempts and some progress is being made – whilst this is happening surely many of the local branches of these associations should aim to have joint meetings and co-ordinated policies. There is much common ground to interest and benefit all; expenses could be saved by having joint speakers, ideas could be swapped and discussed and differences sometimes resolved.

Development of playcentres
Day nurseries and the few nursery centres that exist have reflected the realization that provision for some under-fives geared to three school terms with long holidays in between is just not adequate. Most young children are at a loss when it comes to school holidays – some parents are equally at a loss, particularly when their home and local environment is inadequate for the play needs of children. Some community schemes have started playcentres for children to run during the school holidays. Many local authorities have announced a policy of 'dual use of premises' and are in agreement for these schemes to be held on school grounds subject to the approval of the headteacher. As yet, playschemes have tended to be aimed at the primary and secondary aged child – hopefully the under-fives will be catered for, and again the nursery unit with its scaled down equipment is the ideal base. I am not suggesting that nursery teachers or their assistants should be the people to run holiday playschemes – their work during the term will be exhausting and time for refreshment is essential. Maybe they should be involved in the planning of such schemes and in advising the panel of volunteers who plan to run the project. This is another opportunity for mothers to help run ventures for their own children. Once given the initial support and encouragement to start a play session in a very small way with a few children, confidence will increase and many more joint holiday activities can spread from this. Instead of feeling trapped and isolated with their demanding young families during the holidays, a few mothers will be encouraged to plan outings and organize games, and through this comes the realization of joint enjoyment and a sense of satisfaction in 'coping'.

THE NURSERY UNIT AND THE HOME
This final section is to my mind the most important. If we are to have

any relevance to the community, surely we must work in a way that is understandable and meaningful to the homes of our small children. In order to explore this aspect of the work, perhaps it is worthwhile to look at the major reasons for a nursery communicating with and working with parents.

The argument on the importance of environment as opposed to heredity in development continues. The pendulum is now slowly swinging away from the belief that nearly all is due to acquired characteristics, and there is a feeling that we should pay more attention to the genetic contribution. However, it is now generally accepted that development of intelligence is accounted for by the interaction of the environment with genetic influences. There is also evidence to show that the environment will affect a child most during periods of rapid development. The time of most rapid growth is during the early years and so we can assume that this is when he is going to be most affected by his home and all that it has to offer. We often describe a child's development in terms of stages – each stage must be built upon the basis which has already been established – so it is with the home and the school. When a child enters a nursery unit he is bringing with him three or four years of experience gained from his parents and siblings. This experience is going to continue throughout his schooldays, and if we regard it as irrelevant, or even as an unfortunate influence which is as far as possible to be erased by the ethos of the school, then we are attempting to deal with a child in a void – one who has no previous developmental platform. How can we hope to have any measure of success if we ignore or try to eradicate previous roots – roots which will continue to grow strongly whatever is attempted in school?

Secondly entry into the nursery is often a sensitive time. In the highly mobile, nuclear family of today it is likely that the child is leaving his family for the first time to emerge into another world of different people who have different expectations from those of his parents. From the parent's point of view this may initially be an upsetting time, and this may be reinforced if the child shows some initial reluctance to settle in the nursery. Any parental anxiety will transmit itself to the child, and if it is not dealt with promptly and sympathetically, the entire family may suffer rather than benefit from the offer of a nursery placement. Close liaison between the nursery teacher, parent and child can prevent much of this anxiety, and indeed can work to make the introduction to the school system a joyful occasion. This is a favourable educational start.

The third reason for working with parents is to provide a service. I am not referring just to matters narrowly concerned with the school environment: clearly teachers will need to make it known that children need wellington boots and gloves at school – some parents will readily send these articles, others will ignore the request. In the last analysis the important thing is that the child has dry feet and warm hands, and rather than indulging in disapproving comments about 'inefficient mothers' it is more practical to keep spare wellington boots and gloves at school. More important is the fact that most parents do worry about their young children, and this worry is common at all levels of society. Many young mothers in particular have considerable pressures upon them — high standards of housework, the need to go out to work to contribute to the family income, and the dual role of wife and mother. Trying to do justice to all these demands inevitably brings conflicts, and if the child starts showing some behaviour difficulties (sometimes simply as a result of normal development) mothers will react badly to these symptoms and there is sometimes danger of breakdown of relationship between the parents and the child.

Katherine Read sums up:

In working with parents there are two main goals. The first is to help parents grow in confidence. The parent who feels confidence in himself or herself is better able to enjoy his child and to realize an intuitively wise use of the experiences they have together. The confident parent is better able to learn about the needs of children. He or she is likely to use this knowledge more effectively.

The final reason is the importance of seeking to improve the quality of future parents. Kellmer Pringle observes that:

Modern parenthood is too demanding and complex a task to be performed well merely because we all have once been children ourselves. Those who have been deprived of adequate parental care, thus not having had an opportunity to observe even those parental skills which were practised a generation ago, have little chance of becoming in turn responsible parents themselves.

If we are to do anything to stop the 'cycle of deprivation' we must accentuate the importance of parenthood and its accompanying duties and rewards. The nursery can play an important part in this programme of education. Let us now look at ways in which nursery units can help to exploit home influence and develop relationships with parents.

We have seen certain evidence pointing to the great importance of the first years, even before a child enters a nursery — at the end of the first three years certain patterns of development have been ineradicably established. It makes sense to look at this period of babyhood and see what assistance and guidance can be given to the parents to make them aware of their crucial role as the child's first educators. They must be helped to see that through the daily battle of wills, the frustrations and strains of coping with a young child his very significant pattern of development is emerging. The health visitor helps the mother by visiting the home and being present at clinics to advise on physical development. Many health visitors have extended their role and are dealing with the whole child and his place in the family, rather than merely his physical needs. What is perhaps needed is some educational equivalent to the health visitor to develop a relationship with the parents from the time that the baby is born and to provide continual support for the family as the child's emotional and educational needs develop – preparing for his entry into a nursery at three years.

A scheme similar to this was tried and well received. Part of the E.P.A. project in the West Riding of Yorkshire was to provide a trained teacher as a pre-school home visitor for twenty children between the ages of eighteen months and four years. All the children were assessed by a psychologist and the home environment was evaluated in certain ways (e.g. what toys were available). The children were visited for one to two hours weekly. On each occasion specific toys were provided and their use and value was carefully explained to the mother, after which they were left in the home. Between each visit parents were encouraged to use these toys with their child. A few other authorities have adopted the home visitor scheme and have attached them to large council housing estates where there are an abundance of very young children.

The clear advantage of this scheme is that, with skilled support, the parent is learning to work with the child. The delight of the parent as responses are elicited from the child only serves to reinforce the parent/child relationship. This must be the basis of sound development progress for any child.

There are two main difficulties to the wide establishment of this type of worker. The first is clearly expense; at a time of economic stringency we cannot afford to add further heavy burdens to our pre-school programme. The appointment of one or two full-time trained home visitors is a luxury that not many authorities feel that they could manage at the present. The second drawback is the problem of finding a person with the right qualities and background for this work. Clearly the home visitor must have some teaching qualification relevant to small children. Equally clearly, she must be able to enter many different types of homes and build up good rapport with the adults in them. To be able to do the latter successfully implies that some social work training may be desirable. Unfortunately, there are not many trained teachers who are qualified in social work.

Looking at these difficulties it would still be possible to provide a home visitor service if we look once more to our nursery unit. As we have seen the trained nursery teacher is the expert with young children and by the nature of her job already does have constant and good relationships with parents if she is working properly. She does not have a social work background, but as the entire syllabus of the nursery teachers' training is being closely looked at at present, perhaps a relevant option could be introduced into the training programme. A one-term course on home-visiting would seem useful to all nursery teachers dealing with parents – whether or not in the home. By providing relevant training for the nursery teacher she becomes the one person suited for home visitor work. However, the Local Authority pay the teacher to be in the nursery unit during the day – when is she to be released to visit the homes of younger siblings? There are two possibilities – first the teacher who is appointed to do home visiting as part of her job should expect to work after school for at least two afternoons a week (after all, many primary and secondary teachers take extra-curricular clubs as part of their work in school). Alternatively the teacher could be released for a half day a week to go visiting and during this time the nursery nurse would be in charge of the unit with additional assistance from students in school or the loan of an auxiliary from another class. Both of these proposals have drawbacks and require considerable enthusiasm to put them into practice, but they are feasible. It is also important that there is clear recognition of the responsibility for home-visiting and the nursery teacher who agrees to do this should be given a high scaled post in the school (in the case of a separate nursery school the home visiting would usually be done by the head teacher).

The fact that the nursery teacher is appointed as a home visitor does have one big advantage – she will be well known to the child by the time he is ready to enter the nursery unit, and this brings us to the second reason for close relationship – a need for a sensitive approach to the young child starting school for the first time.

Katherine Read comments:

The way the mother really feels about sending the child to nursery school will have a profound effect on the way the child adjusts there. If she feels reluctant, or unsure or over anxious about his attending, she hinders his accomplishment of the task of meeting the new experience and growing more independent.

Let us now look at the way in which a child may enter nursery school and what is needed to ensure a successful settlement.

Whether a systematic home visiting scheme is established or not, it is important that the child's first meeting with his nursery teacher should be on home ground where he is feeling confident and in control of the situation. The mother may well have mixed feelings about sending her child 'away', albeit for a few hours a week. Her own mother didn't do it and possibly disapproves (and even if grandparents live some distance away their attitudes may still influence a family) and it does mean coming to terms with the child growing up and becoming less dependent. A great deal of reassurance may have to be given to both parent and child. The initial home visit need not be long or arduous, but should be sufficient to set the home/school liaison on a good footing, and to suggest a date when parents and child could come along for a first visit to the school.

The school visit should be another relaxed occasion with time for conversation over a cup of coffee. For many parents this will be the first time they have crossed over the school threshold since they were at school, and this can have an inhibiting effect, particularly if their school memories are not happy ones. An introductory leaflet containing all relevant information about the unit can be on hand. This prevents the need for too many facts and figures to be introduced during the early meetings – they are not absorbed if given orally but should be available for parents.

During the first school visit a small child will usually be content to stay close to mother whilst absorbing the atmosphere around him. He should be shown around the unit and again with mother nearby he should be allowed to investigate at leisure. Some children may wish to browse quietly in the book corner, always considered a 'secure' area. Others may confidently rush off to join the nursery group – each child should be given the opportunity to go at his own pace and both parent and child must feel that they are in a welcoming establishment.

During the initial visit it is important that the mother is reassured about not having to abandon her child at the school door each day. It is recognized that making the break from the immediate family is a big step for a three-year-old and can only be done satisfactorily if gradual steps are taken towards separation. Certainly, if at all possible mother should remain at school throughout the first session, and for the most part of the second. She may then be wise to leave for short periods each day, making sure that the child understands that she will return promptly with the other mothers at the end of the day. Initially the newcomer will wish to remain close to one adult who will act as a mother substitute. It is necessary that the same adult be prepared to keep him by her side for the first few days – later he will be ready to share his attentions amongst other adults present and then to play happily with his peers.

This may sound a very laborious process for accepting a child into a school environment but it is worth remembering that only the truly secure child will be capable of emotional stability and self-reliance. The early years of childhood are the time to ensure that the individual is capable of leading his own life independently in a suitable setting for a short time each day – when the time comes for infant school and the learning of skills, this independence will be well established.

I recognize whilst writing this that there are many parents and children who do not fit into the outlined descriptions. Some mothers will be only too happy to use the nursery for their own convenience and will not be consistent in bringing their own children. Some will not be prepared to work in partnership with the school for the sake of their child. We will never establish the ideal relationship with every parent, many of whom are finding the strains of life so great that they feel inadequate as people in their own right. The teacher can but show the parent that the child's happiness and development is all important to her and because of this the parent is regarded as an important person in the process.

When a child first starts at the nursery we hope that both parent and teacher are working towards the same goal – that of settling the child into the group. What of this parent teacher relationship when the goal has been established and the child no longer requires his mother's presence in the unit? The playgroup movement has shown us that there is an important place for parent participation in a pre-school unit. In particular young mothers of first children do need their confidence boosting about their ability to rear their children. The early years of life are a glorious energy-packed time for the child, but not the easiest for a mother to cope with – yet she does *not* want her job taken away from her. Most parents, if they are honest with themselves, will admit that their children are the most precious part of them – sometimes, though, this realization is lost when life becomes too stressful. The nursery teacher, as a specialist in the needs of young children, is the person to reveal to the parents the potential of their children, and most important, to make them aware that material considerations apart, they are all capable of being adequate and good parents. How can the nursery teacher achieve this task with the parent when she is already doing a demanding job with the children? I suggest that the means are varied, but that the term to cover them all is 'involvement in the school'. We will look at some of the ways of involving parents and at their effectiveness.

The most obvious way is to formalize the relationship between home and school and have a parent-teacher association. Many primary schools have this type of association but fewer nursery schools, on the grounds that they are unnecessary for such small establishments – they do however often have similar groups with appointed Mothers' committees. These groups have a primary role of fund-raising for the school, often by means of social occasions such as bazaars, beetle drives, or dances. Although this type of involvement may start off on a monetary and social level it quite often spills over into other areas of the school. The association may ask itself what it is fund-raising for – a certain piece of equipment becomes desirable and the teacher can explain why she would like the children to benefit from it. Parents will feel a pride of achievement as they are able to see the equipment and facilities that their own efforts have bought the children. The social aspect is also valuable with parents meeting together and mixing with staff in other than a school setting. Family needs are often communicated and can be dealt with in this type of atmosphere with parent and teacher meeting as social acquaintances. While the professional relationship is a reality and must be recognized as such, it can sometimes hinder communication.

The second way of involving parents does not require any formalized associations and is the quintessence of the community school way of working. This is by assuming and ensuring that parents are welcomed into the school and are *used* in the school.

This welcome needs to be emphasized at the extreme ends of the school day – gradual entry and withdrawal of the children at the end of the day does mean that parents can easily wander into the nursery and stay with their children for a while without any congestion. This freedom is so important for a relaxed feeling amongst parents and they do begin to feel that their childrens' school is a friendly, familiar place.

Unless a parent needs to see a nursery teacher for a certain purpose during the school day, an appointment to visit should be unnecessary; for instance if a working mother has the opportunity to leave work one afternoon and see her child at work in the nursery, she should be able to call into the unit at will. Objections are sometimes raised on the grounds that too many visitors unsettle the children. But if the framework of the nursery is secure and the team of teacher and nursery nurse is constant, then the child is not likely to be unduly disturbed by the presence of other adults – rather, this extra interaction will provide them with more experience of grown-ups.

Having mothers in to help during the school day does require more organization if it is to operate successfully. A rota for mothers to sign is a good idea – even if it is abandoned eventually when certain mothers wish to come in regularly and this becomes accepted. A vague instruction to 'generally help' is just not enough for an adult who may at first feel rather unsure and self-conscious about being with a group of young children. A specific task should be set aside which the teacher feels is geared to the liking and ability of the helper. This can vary from sewing, to dealing with the painting corner, to reading in the book corner. The essential thing is that the helper must feel that she is being of use if she is to benefit. She must also be of use if the teacher is to benefit and both can happen if the task and situation are right. Some mothers, particularly those who are under mental stresses, will not be able to stand the noise and activity of a group of young children – they should be offered some quieter accommodation in an adjoining room if possible – others are confident to be with a group of children immediately. Occasionally a parent will be embarrassed if her child overreacts to her presence in the room – this will disappear in due course, and unless the behaviour is extreme the teacher should try to persuade the parent not to stop coming because of this initial difficulty.

'Parental involvement' is a very overworked and misused term, but it is important and can benefit teacher, parent and child. Once teachers can get used to the idea that a parent helper is not there to usurp her role, but to help extend it, she can add to the scope of her nursery group. By being in the unit and seeing the organization and methods used, the parent should be helped to help her child; good examples are showing how the child will first learn to write in lower case letters and should therefore have his name written in this way, the importance of reading the right type of stories to children, and most important aiding the realization that children do not differ basically and all have simple requirements of love and approval. The child too will gain directly by meeting these other adults, and most of all by knowing that *his* mother has a good relationship with *his* teacher.

Two final theories to dispel about parental involvement. Parents will not be queueing up to become 'involved' – some will not wish to work in the school, some will not be able to because of work outside, some will only tentatively offer after the scheme has been working for some time. Moreover, involvement does not only happen on the school premises. A chat between teacher and mother in the home or in the local shop might have great repercussions in enlightenment and further interest. The degree and success of each parent's involvement with her child's schooling will be in accordance with the contribution that she is able to offer.

The final way for a nursery to work with the home is to direct its attention to the quality of future parents, and by close liaison with young people foster some understanding of young children and what great demands are made on parents today. Any project that will encourage the birth and rearing of a child to be a responsible, planned action will be of the greatest value to the community as a whole.

Many secondary schools today are sending their older pupils to help in playgroups and nursery units in order to provide them with practical experience as part of courses on marriage and parenthood, though it may be questionable how successful such a course can be when aimed at girls and boys who have no immediate intention of becoming parents. Moreover, a girl who has no interest in small children can prove to be a positive hindrance to the teacher or playgroup supervisor, and the girl will gain little from the pre-school environment – however interested she is – if she has not received adequate preparation and some grounding in child development. Having said this it is apparent when looking at some of these schemes that many young people have gained great enjoyment and a store of practical knowledge from being in a nursery and working with the children. Young children do enjoy the company of young adolescents, and the right type of secondary boy or girl can make a good contribution to the unit. One of the best ways to work this type of course is for the nursery teacher or playgroup supervisor to visit the group of secondary pupils at their school and give them an introductory talk about the philosophy and practice of working with young children. Visits to the nursery could then be followed with 'feed-back' sessions with the secondary teacher at school. At the very least these pupils will be able to see that school beginnings are now different from their own experience of ten years previous, and possibly the practical part of the course will enable them to think of young children as 'people'.

Children must be wanted if they are to benefit from adequate mothering in life. Suitable advice on family planning should be based on the same campus as the other social and welfare facilities which are linked with the school. Many young mothers may be capable of dealing with the mainly physical needs of the very young baby, but the increasing demands of parenthood will only dawn gradually as the child develops – by this time, having been lulled into a false sense of confidence, the mother may be pregnant again, and even less likely to cope properly with her toddler.

Mothers with young babies should be encouraged to visit a nursery to prepare them for the next stage in their child's life. In the same way regular talks by a member of the nursery staff to ante-natal groups of mothers would help to give a more realistic picture of what parenthood involves, rather than bathing a plastic doll – which still seems to play an integral part in every motherhood class.

Susan Isaacs, one of our greatest nursery teachers, emphasized the importance of home/school relations but stressed that:

. . . its (the nursery school's) prime function is not to take the place of the home: it is to supplement the normal services that the home renders to its children and to make a link between the natural and indispensable fostering of the child in the home and social life in the world at large.

Part two   Nursery practice

4
The child's behaviour

Accepting that some early educational and social environment to supplement the home is desirable for all young children we must now consider the varied opinions as to what type of environment this should be. Certain premises remain clear. The environment should allow the child to begin to act independently of his family, and therefore some separation from mother is desirable. Some interaction with his peers is considered beneficial, and therefore such an environment should be on a group basis. The proposed environment should be deliberately planned for the children with regard to equipment, organization and activities. Given these three requirements there is then a controversy as to what the content of a nursery course should be: do the children just attend and play freely with equipment, with the trained adult only making sure that they do not harm themselves, or do they use their time in learning formal skills of reading, writing and numeracy that will enable them to forge ahead in the primary school? (This is the type of nursery particularly advocated for socially deprived children by Bereiter and Englemann.)

It will be apparent what type of programme is advocated for the young child in this book, but first let us state our over-riding principle that whatever system is adopted it must benefit the individual child. In the midst of intricate discussions as to whether too much or too little intervention is useful, or what materials are most beneficial for young children, it must be remembered that our aim is to create the most suitable setting for a child in which his growth will flourish. Everything else is academic.

Before we can consider the right type of environment for our very young children, we must look at the various components of behaviour which are within the child and are developing so rapidly during these years. Only by looking here can we start to determine what a child will require in terms of facilities and equipment to aid this development. This section will look generally at the young child's development with special reference to emotional, social, physical and cognitive growth, and then discuss how a nursery setting can be made relevant to these areas.

DEVELOPMENT

Describing the birth experience in 1890, William James said that 'the baby, assailed by eyes, ears, nose, skin and entrails at once, feels it all as one great blooming, buzzing confusion.' Sixty months later (or the equivalent to that stage of development) looking at the same child, we see that he has fluent speech, can play sociably with a group of children and understands the need to share and take his turn. His co-ordination is becoming precise and he can dress and feed himself. Physically he is well developed and is able to hop, skip and run ably, and can almost keep time to music. He is now drawing representational pictures, he can use scissors and can recognize some primary colours and match most other colours. At no other time in a child's life is he developing so rapidly in every direction. Although every individual's development is unique, the developmental process does follow a pattern, and given favourable genetic and environmental conditions will unfold smoothly and soundly.

The controversy over whether hereditary or environmental factors are most important for development continues. Clarke and Clarke state that:

In growth of all kinds, the interaction of powerful genetic forces and powerful environmental forces is at work cumulatively over long periods of development. In optimum environments, genetic factors will appear predominant and environment will appear less important because its influence is roughly constant. In sub-optimum environmental effects will appear more obvious.

It remains clear that genetic factors can only produce the basic potential, and it is environmental conditions that will decide whether that potential is going to be fully developed or remain stunted and crippled. The crucial nature of the early years of life means that environmental conditions play a particularly important part in determining the child's growth and consequently his subsequent development. J W B Douglas in *The Home and the School* (1967) states that the child from the poor home background progressively declines in his school attainment, whereas the reverse is true for the child coming from favourable home circumstances. This is not only true in the narrow field of academic attainment. The results of the 1972 Longitudinal Study from the National Children's Bureau shows the great social, emotional and physical differences existing in children coming from different environments. This research amongst others provides a strong argument for some early intervention and enriched environment, particularly for the disadvantaged child. We will now turn more particularly to the years between two and five, when a child is likely to enter the nursery, and look at the type of development taking place.

Emotional development

The two-year-old is at a turbulent time of his life. He may stamp and scream if he is not allowed to dress himself: Erikson suggests that his sense of autonomy is being attacked, and some satisfactory balance has to be established between the child's freedom and his dependency. This battle is carried out during the second and third year of life. The anger of a three-year-old is fierce and deeply felt, it is aroused by interference with his actions or his possessions, and it is usually expressed in physical terms such as kicking and resisting any bodily restraint. A young child will very easily become tearful when angry, particularly before he is verbally able to express his fury: screams are often a fierce substitute for words. We should not underestimate the strength of a child's anger: in a burst of fury he does really mean that he wishes to cut off his brother's head. Because these feelings are so real for him they should not be ridiculed. At this age he will also have no concept of cause and effect and if his brother does happen to fall and hurt himself, the child may well believe that the force of his temper made this happen. Fortunately this stage of violent temper tantrums begins to dwindle around three and a half: as the child's autonomy becomes established his anger will become more controlled and is less likely to be expressed in such violent terms.

Two and three years are the time when the child experiences a range of intense although brief emotions: this degree of intensity will only be reached again at adolescence when the next crucial growth period is reached. He will feel pleasure and fear very strongly and will respond to these emotions physically: hands squeezed together and hopping with excited anticipation at the thought of a sudden treat, or shrinking into a corner or burying his head in mother's coat if something frightens him. As he gradually comes to understand the force of his emotions and to cope with them the total physical reaction will not be quite so visible: the five-year-old is a much more contained person, still liable to excitement and fears, but controlling them more.

At two years the child's main attachments will be to his family, and to his mother in particular. He may not be ready to tolerate a separation from his mother until he is three years or even older. No firm rules can be stated here as the child's ability to extend his environment without mother will depend so much on his previous experience, whether he has been used to mixing with other adults and children, and his own personality. Most children experience some reluctance when leaving their mother for the first time, and Gesell wisely suggests that this process should be treated as gradually as weaning, with special reference to a child's needs.

The small child is a warm friendly personality with an inclination to form strong likings for any adult who takes a close interest in him. His affections are physically demonstrable, he likes to touch and stroke his teacher, and will want to hold her hand if going for a walk. His strongest affections will still of course be kept for his mother, and Erikson suggests that a child's development of his sense of trust will only spring from his earliest experiences of a satisfactory relationship with his mother. The most satisfactory start for the child to develop independent attitudes is that based on the security of his own relationships at home. If these initial bonds are not formed, then the child can be likened to a rootless plant: a sad example of this is children in residential homes whose mothering is undertaken by various members of staff who come and go on shift duty. A visitor to such a home is likely to be inundated by bids for attention: these are children who indiscriminately and greedily look for affection, but are often incapable of developing social traits themselves or later of forming satisfactory relationships with their peers. Kellmer Pringle suggests that on a child's need for love 'depend the healthy development of the personality, the ability to respond to affection, and in time to become a loving, caring parent'.

Finally, the healthy young child is dominated by curiosity. Whereas the very young baby does not show much interest apart from satisfying his bodily needs, the child of three is consumed by the desire to find out about himself, about other people, and anything that is happening in the environment which he happens to be in. He needs to explore his own body and to compare his physical makeup with that of his peers, and he needs to be provided with a sufficiently varied environment to stimulate this curiosity.

This curiosity manifests itself in constant questioning and experimenting to find an answer. It is a strong emotion, and all young children possess it to some degree, but if it has not been nurtured in early life, this essential ingredient for motivation will be stunted and the child will not learn so efficiently. Curiosity will slowly die if questions are constantly discouraged, if experimenting is equated with naughtiness, and if the surroundings are very monotonous. Conversely it will blossom if encouraged and if a rich environment is provided on which curiosity can feed.

Social development

However academically able an individual may be, life cannot be satisfactory for him if he is unable to integrate in society to some degree and have a working relationship with his peers. The child's earliest years are the time for introducing him to society and giving him his first experiences of group situations. Erikson's description of the child's search for autonomy when he is establishing that he is a person in his own right, is opposed to the socialization process which is beginning in the home as parents encourage and expect their child to conform to certain situations: this conflict which arises around the second and third year of life results in the child adopting negative behaviour (see p 60). Once the child has established his autonomy, the process of socializing becomes slightly easier, and this is confirmed by Piaget's assertion that during the child's pre-operational period of development (that is approximately between two and seven years of age) he is gradually learning to differentiate between himself and the world: the child of under two is unable to view himself as a separate entity.

After the age of two the presence of other children becomes increasingly important to the young individual, and with the development of language the beginnings of social growth are seen. Although the start of socialization is seen within the family, the child really needs to be in the company of his peers before he can truly develop as a social being. The limits of a child's sociability are not seen clearly until he is observed with other children in a play situation. Play will be discussed at a later stage, here we are considering it in purely social terms. At the age of two years a child will have reached the stage of *Parallel Play*. He is still at Piaget's egocentric stage of development, but enjoys having other children around him. There is little or no interaction in a play situation, but children of this age will play alongside one another using similar equipment.

The next stage is one of *Associative Play*, when at about three years of age children will be observed playing together in a group situation, but there is in fact no sharing of interests. They may borrow ideas from one another, but will be carrying out their independent roles.

There is some dispute as to what age a child is able to join in true *Cooperative Play*. Piaget suggests that this stage is not reached until the child is seven or eight years old. Gesell's findings pointed to American children playing co-operatively two or three years earlier. It may well be that different nursery environments were being studied, and that Piaget was watching children playing in a Montessori based nursery where children work with materials more on an individual basis. Cooperative play involves the children being able to play together in a group situation, sharing ideas, taking turns and making joint decisions. Margaret Wood (1973) suggests that children who know one another well are likely to attain cooperative play at a much earlier age, and this would have implications for a nursery situation particularly where children attended on a full-time basis for one or two years before First School.

Let us now look at the young child as a developing social being and note some of his personality traits.

Negativism, as we have mentioned, is linked with the child

establishing his individuality and is seen in its strongest form in the two and three-year-old. Although recognized as part of the pattern of normal development, the behaviour is often very trying for the adult who is coping with it. The child may become stubborn and resistant to suggestion. The word 'no' is frequently used and requests from an adult frequently refused. Negative behaviour will also include emotional displays of temper tantrums and destructiveness. The behaviour is usually accentuated when an adult makes direct demands upon a young child, when impatience or intolerance is shown towards a child's slowness or initial clumsiness. Whenever the child feels pressurized in this way he will resort to negativism. As he matures and establishes his autonomy, negativism will decline and the need for social approval will become increasingly important. Hurlock (1972) suggests that a young child is at first unable to differentiate between social approval and attention, and if he is not able to obtain the first he will resort to various types of attention-seeking behaviour which may be unacceptable (shouting, aggression, hiding). The child grows to learn that not all of this behaviour is socially acceptable, and starts to regulate his actions. In time the need for social approval and the growth of his cooperative play means that the four and five-year-old is able to take part in and benefit from occasional group situations: these will occur informally through his play, and in a more structured way when organized by the teacher. It is only by being in a group situation that an individual will learn in time to cooperate, to share and to take turns.

Aggression is a very necessary driving force, which, in order to promote healthy development, must be channelled positively. Hostile aggressive behaviour in young children is generally agreed by psychologists to be a result of some frustration. Joan Cass says that this frustration occurs both towards people and objects:

. . . objects because they get in the way, or will not behave as the child wishes: parents and other adults because they are frustrating and demanding. They expect him to do things he does not want to, and they deny him pleasures he feels he has a right to enjoy.

Whereas the three-year-old will mainly show aggression by use of physical force, the five-year-old will have more control over his physical outlets and greater verbal ability: aggression develops into quarrelling and teasing. Despite this, young children are basically friendly, and where the aggressors are reasonably evenly matched, battles are usually resolved amiably and no resentment exists. A certain degree of aggression from children at this age should be accepted sympathetically as the child matches himself against the outside world. But intervention is necessary where the aggression is pointed at a less able individual and develops into bullying. The bully figure is the insecure young child or the badly adjusted child who has some speech difficulty or other handicap which causes him to feel inadequate and unable to assert himself against an equal. In this case the remedy needs to be sought for the handicap which causes the bullying rather than just preventing the attack.

Finally we can view the first five years of life as a time of growth from the totally dependent new born-baby who looks to its mother for all its needs to the independent figure of the five-year-old who is capable of making conscious decisions and carrying them out. This process of growth towards self-autonomy is very important. We all know the drag on the community that an over-dependent adult can prove to be, and the earliest possible encouragement needs to be given to enable the young child to start regulating his own actions and to become responsible for his actions. We have already mentioned that satisfactory independent growth cannot take place unless roots of affection and security have first been established in the home: however the secure home background should not suppress the small child's inborn instinct to want to do things for himself. If he is not allowed to try for himself and to occasionally make mistakes, he will eventually not wish to try and will become over-dependent. Training the child to be self-regulating should be a purposive and gradual process, as with everything else the building will only take place on the structure that has been established already at home.

When we look at the social and emotional growth of the young child it is clear that these two aspects of development go hand in hand, and any disturbance of one will affect the other. The emotionally unstable child who is unable to control temper tantrums or who is withdrawn and uncommunicative is unlikely to form satisfactory social relationships with his peers. We can also see that these early years are the time when sound emotional growth is being established and social attitudes are being formed. The young child searches for social contact, but may lack the skill of making it: as he is gradually weaned away from his mother his independence grows, and his diminishing egocentricity allows him to cooperate in a group. All these foundations are being laid by the time the child finishes his nursery schooling.

Physical development

A child's bodily growth and the way in which he uses his body will have a very real effect on the way he operates in his environment. Healthy physical development is a prerequisite to satisfactory learning: a child whose body hurts or bothers him, or whose muscles will not function efficiently is unlikely to greet new experiences enthusiastically and will be more vulnerable emotionally. The child's developing perceptions are dependent initially on his physical interaction with the world around him: if he is limited physically his perceptions will be affected. Examples of this are seen with the spina bifida child who cannot lift objects and will consequently find it difficult to acquire a concept of weight, and the blind child whose inability to visualize must be compensated for in other sensory directions.

The child's stature and physical build may also affect him, particularly if his growth deviates from the norm, resulting in an obese or extremely thin physique. A balanced diet and physical exercise are important to help ensure that a child's weight is in due proportion to his height, although sometimes abnormalities may occur, because of emotional or psychosomatic disorders.

Although the pre-natal period and the first three years of life are the most rapid period of growth for the child (the next being puberty) the years between two and five do see physical development. Between these years a child will normally grow six inches in height and will increase approximately thirteen pounds in weight. The growth of the nervous system is very rapid in the pre-natal period and during the first four years of life. The brain increases in size mainly during these years: by the age of four the child's brain will measure four-fifths of its adult weight.

The early years of life are all important for developing control of the body muscles or motor control. Katherine Read states:

A child builds self-confidence from control of his muscles. He gains when he is in tune with his own body, able to use it freely following his own rhythm. His posture and the way he uses his body reveal attitudes about himself. The child with good motor skills can do more about what he perceives. He has more confidence as he plays with other children and copes with situations.

The physical process of development from the helpless, uncoordinated newborn baby to the agile, energetic and independent five-year-old is a compressed and orderly one. Normally one stage will be completed successfully before another can begin, and as with all aspects of development the rate of progress will vary according to the opportunities that the child has to acquire these skills.

When looking at physical development it is necessary to note the difference in the rate of progress between boys and girls. Most surveys show that boys are considerably slower to develop fine motor movement and this will reflect on his ability to dress himself, and later to begin to write.

If we consider Mary Sheridan's (1968) chart of development for young children we can acquire some idea of his growth of competence in fine and gross motor skills. The three-year-old is beginning to dress himself and will wash his hands but not bother about drying them. He can eat tidily, but still finds use of a knife difficult. By five years these social skills are carried out easily and competently. Given the opportunity the three-year-old will draw with a pencil and use paint liberally on an easel. Representational pictures do not usually occur until he is about four years old and around five years the child's hand control should be good enough for him to start to form letters (clearly this is dependent on whether he has had sufficient practice in the use of crayons, pencils and brushes). The range of a child's gross motor movements follow on from his learning to walk. At first the three-year-old will need to concentrate when running, and his attempts may end in a fall. By five years the child is agile and will be able to run as part of a game. The three-year-old will be able to throw a ball, but will not be able to catch until some time later. Between the years of three and five the child will learn to skip, balance, hop and dance to music. All these skills will require some guidance, encouragement and the opportunity to practise.

Cognitive development
This is the final aspect of a child's development and has been deliberately kept to last, because satisfactory cognitive development is dependent upon social, emotional and physical growth. It is in fact impossible to separate one facet of growth from another, all are interdependent and interweave to produce the healthy, competent, curious five-year-old who will embark on his statutory school career.

As we look at the development of a child's understanding or his acquisition of concepts we will pay particular attention to Piaget's work. Although other psychologists have investigated this aspect of development Piaget has done the most important work so far as the young child is concerned. Piaget states that from birth to seven years a child will go through stages of development. This development starts with the newborn baby having no understanding of his environment and possessing only reflex actions, and it unfolds until at seven years of age (or the developmental equivalent) a child is able to organize his experience into a whole and to think logically so long as his thinking is linked to concrete objects. Although we are not directly concerned with the extremes of this developmental age range it will be useful to place our nursery years in perspective and so we will start with the baby.

The Sensori-motor Stage (from birth to two years)
During this first stage the baby will react to his environment entirely in accordance with his own physical needs – his developing perception and the workings of his body are operating simultaneously. He can suck and swallow and evacuate, and soon after this he learns

to discriminate in such matters as what he is able to suck and what not. His body becomes more coordinated and his behaviour gradually becomes purposive as he is able to repeat his actions voluntarily. A six month old baby will realize that by shaking his rattle he is capable of making a pleasant noise. A few months later he starts to develop some idea of permanence – before this time if a ball was shown to him and then hidden under a cloth the baby would take no further interest in it assuming that the ball was no longer there: now if the ball is shown and then covered he will lift the cloth to look for it as he is starting to understand that it has only been concealed temporarily. During this first stage of concept development the baby has no idea of anything happening outside himself – his concept of time is 'now' and of space is 'here'. He is starting to approach his second phase of development when he anticipates the path of a thrown ball which lands out of his sight. Although his language has not yet developed he is starting to build up pictures in his mind about actions – his thoughts are becoming *internalized*.

The Pre-operational stage (from two to seven years)
As the child approaches this stage he is starting to see himself as separated from his world – things can exist without him and he is learning to internalize more and more of his actions. This process develops rapidly as a child acquires use of language and Piaget has subdivided his pre-operational stage into two periods: from two to four years or the *Pre-conceptual* phase and from four to seven years or the *Intuitive* phase.

During the *Pre-conceptual* phase when the child is learning to use language he will indicate that he is able to think symbolically. His waking time is mainly taken up with play and his imitative play will demonstrate this use of symbolism – he will use a cardboard box for a house or a toy vehicle for his father's car. The child will start to explore his world in the wider context, and discover what is in it – he will do this through his play, and at first the information that he gathers will be somewhat haphazard and will await organization at a later stage.

The second or *Intuitive* phase of the pre-operational stage is the time when the child is having contact with others – this socialization helps to reduce his egocentric approach to the world. During this time the child will tend to make judgements based on his perception of a situation – he is still unable to reason or to think logically, although he is now really able to think in that he is able to verbalize his thoughts. The well known experiment showing the child's use of intuition in his observations is the one when water is poured from one container into a differently shaped container – the child will then say that there is a different level of water in the second container. In the same way the child at the intuitive stage of development, though able to count, has not yet acquired a concept of 'number' – his thinking is still largely influenced by the appearance of things: if six eggs are placed on a table and spaced out more widely than six accompanying eggcups the child will be convinced that there are more eggs on the table than eggcups. His opinion will remain unchanged even if he has previously fitted the six eggs into these eggcups without any being left over.

It is important to remember that Piaget's stages of development are only for the approximate age of child given – critics have suggested that his age groups are too high for the level of attainment suggested, but even if we accept this there can be no disputing Piaget's findings that concept development in a child of whatever ability follows a definite and constant pattern. Muriel Beadle in *A Child's Mind* (1972) sums up Piaget's findings admirably:

Piaget believes that a child's mind is a psychic entity which consistently evaluates by one general mode of thought all the various stimuli which impinge on his consciousness – but that entity, this structured whole, is continually being re-structured by its own interaction with the environment. This means that the thought of infants and children is not a miniature version of adult thought. It is qualitatively different. It changes its form as it 'grows up'.

The most important message from Piaget to us is that in order for a child to acquire concepts he must be given learning opportunities in the form of experience. His concept development cannot be hurried, and indeed it will not progress unless the child is given a chance to discover and test the world and what is in it. The type of experience that he has is also crucial and to make the fullest sense to him it must be direct and concrete. Finally, although at the sensori-motor stage a child starts to develop thought without language having developed it is very soon clear that his ability with language is very relevant to his thought processes. We will look at this question of language in more detail later, but now suffice it to say that during the first five years of life we must aim, as Joan Tough says, for a child to use language as a means of learning.

These then are the four main areas of growth for the young child. No one area is independent of the others and the product both at birth and at the end of the first five years of life is the individual. This individuality is precious. Alice Yardley says that:

. . . a person only knows he lives when he knows he counts as someone special. He requires first and foremost to be needed and respected. There are so many of us that unless we can feel that we matter as separate persons then the life we have is meaningless.

With this dual pattern in mind – the common path of development and the resulting individual we will now look at some situations in the pre-school environment.

DEALING WITH SITUATIONS COMMON TO THE YOUNG CHILD

Settling a child into a nursery environment

Whether a child comes from an advantaged home or not, unless he has attended a Day Nursery (providing extended day care for an age range of nought to five years) his social experiences at three years will have been mainly with adults, with his siblings and possibly with other children on an individual basis. Even if mother works full-time the child is likely to have been left with a childminder who may well only accommodate one or two children during the day. If the minder is interested and involved with the child, the arrangement can be an extension to the child's family life (sometimes even a superior extension if the quality of home life is poor). There are also of course childminders who accommodate far too many children, work on a solely lucrative basis and provide a poor, unstimulating base for a child (see Brian Jackson, 'The Childminder', *New Society*, 29 November 1973). These children will have had a very poor start to life and are some of the priority cases to be considered for nursery placements.

For various reasons the entry into a nursery situation is likely to be traumatic for a young child. If he has been at home with mother for the previous three years one of the most difficult tasks for him will be the initial separation from his parent and home. If he has been with a satisfactory childminder, the pangs of separation will still be there, and in both cases there is the adjustment to being in a group situation and being confronted with a cross-section of one's peers. If the child has already experienced separation from mother and has been in a poorly stimulated group situation such as in some of the overcrowded urban childminders, his main difficulty will be in adjusting to a lively and animated environment, where freedom, mess and conversation and action are not punished, but encouraged. Some children because of their background and parental forethought will be adequately prepared for all these new experiences – some will have difficulty on every front and be faced with an alien environment.

All children to some extent will experience fears of the unknown, of their own inadequacy and of adjusting to a new practical situation full of different adults and children. They will need to lessen their dependence, start developing their social skills and grow in confidence to meet the varied and rich experiences provided in a nursery.

Each child varies in his resources to cope with these requirements. As we have seen, Erikson suggests that the most important initial

71

development in a child is that of building a sense of *trust* in his environment. This will only grow satisfactorily if the individual has experienced a loving and secure start to life, and a special relationship with one adult, whether or not his mother. If we accept this then we can understand that only the truly secure child will be ready to accept happily an extension to his environment which will further his growth. This is the most satisfactory way for a new entrant to a nursery to greet the experience. However one must admit that there are other children who can have had no opportunity to develop their sense of trust and who may have suffered an unsettled and unloved early life, who will enter a nursery and appear to be as settled as the first group. It may well be that these children, although faced with such a different environment will sense that it is in the nursery that they will be able to develop their sense of trust with warm, accepting adults. These are the children who have no initial problems in separating from mother because there are no strong bonds to cut – difficulties may well arise later when the child is still trying to establish this sense of trust in his environment before he can start to experiment and benefit in other ways from the nursery: these are often the children who find socialization and emotional controls so difficult to achieve.

Finally, there are children from disadvantaged and deprived homes, who because of their doubts and tensions will only settle in a nursery after a very long time. Sometimes it is simply that such a child is not yet ready to extend his home situation even though he may be over three years of age: his development is just not yet geared for new experience. Parents and teachers should accept this possibility – a pre-school arrangement must never be allowed to get out of proportion. It is a voluntary decision on the part of the parent to send his child: the experience is designed to enrich the child's environment, to provide a potential source of support for some parents and should be seen as a pleasurable introduction for the family to the school system. If none of these criteria seem to be fulfilled, then the arrangement is valueless.

Starting a child in a nursery involves careful planning and observation. Parents and teacher need to work closely together for as long as the child requires added reassurance and until he has acquired sufficient confidence to adapt.

The best start to the teacher-child relationship is for the initial meeting to be in the child's home (see part 1, chapter 3). As far as possible a child should be able to realize that links exist between his parents and his nursery teacher and between his home and his nursery playroom – every attempt should be made to fuse these into a 'whole' in the child's framework as opposed to conflicting forces pulling him in different directions. If he is able to meet his teacher on familiar ground and see his mother invite her into their home and converse with her, the potential for a trusting relationship has been established. We must also remember that it may not only be the child who is assailed with doubts about entering the nursery. Parents must be reassured that they are not abandoning their child – that the aim of the experience is to build upon the foundations that have already been laid, and that the teacher needs the parents to work with her to ensure the child's wellbeing in the nursery. These are the messages to be communicated during this initial meeting. From the teacher's point of view she will be gathering information about the child (see appendix B) and his home background and generally summing up the relationship between parent and child : all this background will aid her in knowing where to begin when she is working in the nursery situation with the small newcomer.

The home visit will then be followed by the child and one or both parents visiting the nursery and seeing for themselves the building and the organization of the day. The headteacher of a nursery school or a nursery teacher in an attached unit should endeavour to make this a leisurely and relaxed occasion. The parents may well be feeling tense if this is the first time they have stepped over a school threshold since they finished their own school career – their tension may be communicated to the child who will already have quite enough to cope with as he observes the varied activities, the busy, active children, the colour and the strangeness of the situation. He may be excited and eager to join the other children, but at his first visit his predominant emotion will probably be fear, and the younger he is the more likely he is to experience this fearfulness, which will keep him close to mother – cautious and slightly anxious as to what is expected of him. After an initial chat and a look around the nursery, if the teacher senses that the parent is fairly confident she will suggest that parent and child go to look at some of the activities for themselves : left with his parent the child may well start to relax and investigate for himself.

Finally, the child will be accepted onto the nursery register and will start to attend regular sessions. Again it is essential that this is done gradually and initially with the parent present. Even if the placement is for five part-time sessions, a three-year-old may well only benefit from three or four sessions a week at first. For the first term attendance should be geared entirely to the needs of the individual child – the aim should be to increase the sessions until he is attending daily as it is only on the basis of daily attendance that he is really going to benefit from continuity of his play (Parry, 1974). However anxious a child is to start his nursery career he is unlikely to settle immediately.

Sarah ran into the playroom watched by her mother who stood in the doorway. After running a few paces Sarah stopped and surveyed the playroom scene (her eyes widened and her head turned slightly as her glance flickered to the various corners of the room). Her mother called to her: 'I'm going now Sarah, goodbye.' Sarah turned back to her mother and then ran back to the doorway, raising herself on tiptoe to throw her arms around her mother in an attempt to restrain her.

Sarah had been at the nursery for three weeks and her mother had stayed with her for the first week. Even now she was unable to cope with the separation from her mother in the mornings without reluctance and some anxiety.

One of the most common behaviour patterns from a child when starting nursery is overconfidence. The child has been longing to join the nursery and rushes in headlong to join the group. He imperiously tells his mother that he does not need her to stay, and then halfway through the session, the enormity of the situation without her familiar face suddenly hits him and he bursts into panic stricken tears. Such an experience may well badly upset the child and he will be reluctant to attend for the following session. Despite an initial assured exterior the adult should not accept the child's word that he wishes her to leave – of course his independence should be respected, and mother could perhaps retire to another room or busy herself with other children – she should remember however that her child is not yet at a stage of development when he can anticipate events accurately and his emotions are still unpredictable and transitory. Bearing in mind that some mothers are unable to stay with their children because of full-time work pressures or poor mental or physical health (which may be the reason for the child having been granted a priority place at the nursery) it should be an established principle that all mothers who are able are encouraged to stay with their children when they enter the nursery until the child, the parent and the teacher feel that proper adjustment has been made. This may take one day or one month, but it is characterized by the new entrant establishing a sound relationship with one of the adults in the nursery and with him appearing relaxed and interested in his environment on occasions when his mother is not around. Occasionally a parent may attempt to leave her child by creeping out of the nursery unnoticed without saying goodbye. This can badly shake a child's confidence – he has little concept of time anyway and is unable to reason out his mother's disappearance – for all he knows she may have gone for ever. It is important that mother's departure is clearly explained to him and that his mother emphasizes that she will return to collect him from the nursery in time for dinner (or some other familiar part of the day).

The child in the nursery
After gently easing the child into a nursery situation, the adults concerned will heave a sigh of relief when he is happily settled, and

then sit back, allowing the focus of attention to shift slightly from the child. The mother sees that he is happy and this is reward enough for her, and the teacher and nursery nurse will be tending to look more to the other children who may not have had so much attention when the newcomers were settling in. This is how it should be – the child is now confident enough to start interacting with the other adults and children, and to start exploring all the various activities on hand in the nursery. He needs to do this in his own time and gradually establish himself as one of the group.

However, as we have already seen a three or four-year-old is at a sensitive period of development, and when a child of this age is placed in a social environment which provides stimulus and activity deliberately designed to aid his development it is expected that changes will be seen in the child. However advantageous his home, a nursery will add some extra dimension – but of course it is the child from the stultified and barren background who will find such vast differences on his entry to nursery. The sensitive teacher will be aware that this first term in the nursery is a particular time of conflict, of change and adaptation for the child – she will be careful to note changes in behaviour and early developments.

We will look at some of the common developments that may take place when a young child is confronted with a nursery environment.

The social and emotional implications are tremendous – suddenly the child is not one at home but is constantly surrounded by other children. Although there should be sympathetic provision for solitary play in the form of wheeled toys outside and table toys and painting inside, the emphasis is on joint activity and much of the nursery equipment is for group use. One of the early conflicts usually arises over sharing and taking turns. These concepts are alien to many three-year-olds and the teacher will be cognisant of this when she at first intervenes on behalf of the child and then ensures that only occasional demands are made of him. Sharing an adult's attentions may be as difficult for the young child as the sharing of equipment: this again has to be learned gradually and in accordance with the child's needs. Frustrations may still be expressed in the form of temper tantrums which while they last may be violent and destructive and even frighten the child himself. Sometimes a child will enter the nursery tense and withdrawn and often experiences considerable difficulty in separating from mother. This general inhibited behaviour may continue for some time particularly if there is some anxiety-provoking situation at home. With the aid of the adult and with gentle encouragement to participate in activities the child's confidence may increase – sometimes a socially acceptable balance may be achieved, but occasionally the pendulum will swing in the other direction and a previously withdrawn child may develop aggressive tendencies and become generally 'wild' in his behaviour. This may well worry the parent who can only see that her child has 'grown worse' since he started at the nursery. In fact this is all part of development and it is a matter of the child finding the right level of behaviour. Dr Winnicott (1964) observed that:

... because young children of pre-school age tend to be the victims of their own strong emotions and aggressions, the teacher must at times protect the children from themselves and exert the control and guidance necessary in the immediate situation, and in addition ensure the proper provision of satisfying activities in play to help the children to guide their own aggressiveness into constructive channels, and to acquire effective skills.

Perhaps one of the most significant changes in the pre-school child is his move towards independence in the nursery. Erikson mentions that the first strivings for autonomy begin with the toddler and the independent character of a three-year-old will depend — as does so much else — on the type of home environment. Many mothers are busy however or unaware of how important it is to hold oneself back and to allow the child 'to do it for himself, however fumbling and primitive the end result. Opportunities for developing independence must be predominant in every area of the nursery: self-service milk arrangements will allow the individual the chance to pour for himself and to decide what quantity he can drink, convenient toilets mean that the child can go to the lavatory as and when he wishes, the choice to play inside or out with a variety of materials, to attend a story session or not and to select one's playmates are all the beginnings of decision-making for life. A child who is capable of making decisions and acting on his own initiative will grow rapidly in self-confidence.

We have seen that an abundance of physical and motor skills develop in the years before five. The nursery provides opportunity for the children to practise various skills and to be guided in their development. Many small children are reluctant to tackle such apparatus as climbing frames if they have not experienced them before.

They will not tackle any piece of large physical equipment voluntarily unless they are sure that they can cope with it — a child of three and four will exercise caution and careful judgement in his physical play, but he does need to know that an adult is nearby to offer him aid if his confidence suddenly fails him.

The three-year-old has some mastery of both some large and fine motor movements — generally a boy will have superior control of his larger movements and a girl will find finer motor movements easier — both of course will depend on having practised these skills at home.

A new entrant to the nursery will need to be confident enough to learn to use all the facilities within the playroom and the outside area. The nursery garden will hold most of the opportunities for development of large motor movement – the newcomer may watch the other children absorbed in their vigorous play and then gradually join in as his social abilities increase. In the playroom manipulative toys, use of paintbrush and scissors, opportunities for dressing and undressing and using a knife and fork at mealtimes will all develop finer hand movements – as these skills increase with practice so will the child's newly acquired confidence with materials lead him on to further experimentation and developing powers of creativity. He will so delight in his new competence that he will wish to practise and demonstrate at home – these are the delights of learning his first skills away from the home setting.

One particular type of child will gain greatly from a nursery environment offering plenty of outlets for large muscle development – this is the individual with hyperactive or excessively restless tendencies. Hyperactivity is common in many young children, especially boys and those whose homes do not allow the normal necessary outlets for physical energies (e.g. children in high rise flats). Although hyperactive behaviour does not constitute a handicap until the child is much older and then unable to conform to a classroom situation in school, it does cause stress in parents – the young child may be active and energetic without pause throughout the day and sometimes require little sleep at night. When he enters the nursery his needs are predominantly physical, and then after a time his energies are gradually channelled into other forms of play. This sustained opportunity for physical play, and the demands of a new environment should mean that excessive restless behaviour will lessen as the child has his needs met.

Finally, are we likely to see any changes in a child's cognitive development during his early period in the nursery? Most pre-school children are at the Pre-Operational stage of concept development when first actions and then language becomes internalized as their thinking develops. Language development is at a crucial stage here and although it will be discussed later in the book it should be emphasized that with the aid of a skilful teacher the nursery child will be allowed and encouraged to have experiences which are backed and extended by conversation, discussion and enquiry. The language and experience opportunities must go together, and Piaget's findings show us that the experience must be first-hand and practical. Marianne Parry mentions the necessity of finding the most stimulating situations for every child at his point of development – the experiences provided must not be too difficult nor too familiar. Given these 'right' opportunities the child's cognitive foundations should be enriched –

new concepts will develop with new situations – and above all the nursery setting should not only be helping to satisfy his natural curiosity, but to extend it and strengthen his motivation to learn.

5
Play in the nursery

THE ROLE OF PLAY

Having looked briefly at a child's developmental process and his needs, we must now turn to see in practice how a nursery situation will help these needs. First we will say something about the way in which such needs are met through the use of play. This word is overloaded with meaning – it is variously interpreted as wasting time, getting into mischief and enjoying oneself – in fact it rarely involves the first two interpretations but may well mean enjoyment and much more when applied to young children's activity. Educationalists, philosophers and psychologists have all been concerned with the nature of play. Froebel was one of the first to recognize its value in pre-school methodology and Susan Isaacs describes it as 'nature's means of individual education. Play is indeed the child's work and the means whereby he grows and develops.' The philosopher Herbert Spencer described play as a 'manifestation of surplus energy', and Karl Groos, a German philosopher, defined it in 1899 as the practice of skills. Professor Groos went on to say that play had no part in the life of simpler species whose life pattern was already established at birth, but the more complex and intelligent the species the more it needs an initial period of life to imitate and then develop behaviour for future living.

Whilst accepting that all these interpretations have some validity, it may be most sensible for our purpose to consider how a child would exist without the means to play. If we look at the young baby and the early interaction with his mother and his environment we see that after meeting his basic needs, the remainder of his activity can best be described as play. Simple games, songs, introduction to noises and baby toys are all offered to stimulate the child and to encourage his further development. If these were withdrawn the beginnings of language and perception would be severely limited. From birth the young baby needs to explore first his own and his mother's body, then his immediate surroundings. His internal physical development is largely unfolding regardless, but if there is no means for the toddler to find out about materials – if he is not allowed to move, to push, to build and to create noise and mess he will be unable to find out what his world is about and how it relates to him. If his language does not develop, neither his powers of thought nor his imagination will grow, and if he is deprived of what is perhaps the most important age of play when social relations are developed, he will have no opportunity to become a socialized being. Looked at in this light, there can be no satisfactory child development without the aid of play. As the total development of the child is the very *raison d'être* for the nursery its system depends mainly on providing and structuring the resources whereby children can best play.

We have seen that the child's development is interrelated – social, emotional, physical and cognitive growth occur simultaneously, and therefore we cannot plan for one aspect of growth without considering the others. When looking at provision of activities in the nursery we shall see that although they may be under one label they help the child develop in different ways. Thus dramatic play, whilst developing the child's imaginative powers, may also be cementing social and emotional growth and aiding language development. Whilst we will be discussing play under convenient headings it is necessary to remember that most types of play add various dimensions to a child's growth, and one cannot be said to be more important than another. What is important is for the adult to provide a balance of activities to ensure that during his time at the nursery, a child has the opportunity of becoming involved in different circumstances, with different materials at different levels of development. Only in this way will the child be allowed to grow through play.

SOCIAL AND EMOTIONAL PLAY

Imaginative activities

'Make-believe' has an almost magical allure for young children, who love to pretend to be anything from wild animals to giants. The greatest attraction lies in taking on the role of an adult – by being 'grown-up' the young child is attempting to understand and to bring the outside adult world into his frame of reference. Grown ups are all powerful to three and four-year-olds, and often involve them in fearful situations such as parental rows, hospital and dental treatment. If a child can imagine himself to be the angry parent, or doctor or dentist, many of his unspoken fears about these situations may be gradually overcome and eventually conquered. Dramatic play may also allow the individual to express words and actions that would not normally be socially acceptable – it is quite permissible for the doll to be cursed and beaten, and at the same time the small mother in the home corner may be playing out the aggression that she feels towards her baby brother. Such activity may therefore aid adjustment to difficult life situations experienced by the child – it will also help to instil confidence and security in children who are still uncertain of the world and to whom fantasy and reality tend to become intermingled. During imaginative activities the child may play symbolically – a woolly dog may do for a baby and a brick for a bed, although as he grows older this symbolism will lessen and it becomes more important to have more realistic props to hand.

Building a den and playing at mothers and fathers is an age old game for children and one of which they never tire. There should be some provision in the playroom for a flexible home corner and this is best arranged by sectioning off a corner of the room by means of storage units. This corner should be spacious enough to allow for varied movement of two or three children, the partitioning should be stable, for the children should not have to worry about hazards from a flimsy structure and finally the partition should be high enough to allow the children an illusion of privacy, but should still enable the adult to see and hear any action that is taking place within. The quality of language in imaginative play is often freer and more uninhibited than when the child is conversing with an adult – for this reason the adult needs to be aware of it as an aid to his picture of the child's all round development.

Inside the home corner there should be basic pieces of equipment – preferably multipurpose in use. A rug, tables and chairs, small camp bed, cooker and dresser are sufficient, with a full-length mirror either on a stand or fixed to the wall. Although furniture can be kept to a minimum, there should be attention to details: an attractive cover to the bed, matching cups and saucers and cutlery and a tablecloth – far from being unnecessarily fussy, these details will attract a child to the corner and will encourage sustained play, whereas an assortment of odds and ends will be used aimlessly or not at all.

The home corner may be transformed into a hospital, dental surgery, hairdressers, post-office, supermarket or general office in turn. Each change of scene demands certain realistic pieces of equipment and the emphasis should be on improvisation. A relevant interest table or pictures and posters pinned up nearby will help to set the scene. Provision for hospital play for instance would include a bed and cover, a table and chair with notebook and pencil and one or two dolls for patients (often one of the children will volunteer to be the patient and the bed should be strong enough for this). Dressing up clothes should include a nurse's outfit, and a couple of men's shirts for the doctors' coats. The doctor's bag should be well stocked with bandages, stethoscope, disposable masks, plastic syringes, wooden spatulas and various bottles filled with coloured water for medicine.

A general dressing up corner should be situated in or near the home corner. Again it is important that the clothes are displayed attractively.

Ideally clothes should be on coat hangers which are suspended on a low rail, or garments can have loops sewn on to them and then can be hooked onto pegs which are fixed onto the wall. What clothes should be provided? Briefly anything that lends itself to role playing, and this does not necessarily mean that all the clothes should be exotic. Variety is important – long and short dresses in interesting designs and textures, possibly something shimmering with sequins or trimmed in velvet – jackets, cloaks and boleros with a glittering belt to attract small boys. Uniforms of all kinds should be seized upon and duly altered – hats provide an instant way of assuming a role – policeman's and fireman's helmets, caps and souwesters are all ideal. Accessories are also important: wigs (bought or home-made from dyed cottonwool or rope or thick plaited wool), gloves, spectacle frames, razors, walking sticks and babies' bottles all give rise to imaginative play. Particularly appreciated is a decorated box filled with any disused and cheap jewellery.

Imaginative play will of course have no confines and will spill out to all areas of the nursery. Provision should be made outside – a disused car or boat in the grounds can cost very little and provide hours of pleasure. Both have attendant risks and should be made safe for the children by experts. If one is fortunate enough to have a tree large enough to accommodate a safe tree house, then this is the ideal outside home area or den – good substitutes may be found in a wigwam or old caravan, and a pile of large pieces of wood will encourage the children to make their own house. A steering wheel and wooden box may be eagerly converted into a car and a tractor tyre into a ship. The possibilities for imaginative creations are limitless and the limits should only be set by the children.

Play with puppets is an excellent outlet for the imagination and a good means of encouraging language in the more inhibited child. The following ideas are given to illustrate different ways of presenting puppets.

a The teacher may demonstrate use of a puppet by using one as a visual aid to her story, or when talking to a group of children using a puppet to encourage the group to ask questions and to participate in rhymes and songs.

b A box of assorted puppets may be set out for the children with some simple structure for them to use as a theatre: this can be the back of the piano, two chairs covered with a sheet or a converted cardboard box. Puppets can include finger puppets, glove puppets and stick puppets. (See A R Philpott, *Let's Make Puppets*, Evans, 1972).

c Having had some experience with ready made puppets, the older children may like to make their own puppets. These should be *very* simple, the main idea being to give guidance in the basic technique of sticking on features and then providing a range of materials for the child to make his own. Plain brown paper bags are good for hand puppets and yoghourt pots or paper cups stuck onto pieces of doweling will suffice for stick puppets.

d A Christmas party or end of term celebration is an excellent occasion for entertaining the children with a simple puppet show performed by adults. The children can be encouraged to participate in the performance and it is a good way of introducing them to dramatic performances.

Scaled down toys are mainly commercially produced and include miniature farms, zoos, doll's houses and garages. Such toys are expensive but so long as they are tough and durable they are a good investment, particularly as a reassuring starting point for newcomers and as a means for the adult to stimulate conversation with the more withdrawn child.

Although a child may indulge in imaginative play from as early as two years old this is only in an individual form and socialized dramatic play will develop in the later years in the nursery. Here lie great opportunities for practising cooperation, sharing, leading and following and all other requirements that go to making a successful group.

CREATIVE ACTIVITY

Use of natural materials

The world around us provides us with various materials with which to experiment in the form of water, sand, clay, dough, mud and wood. The need to use these materials is very strong, and many adults who do not have the opportunity to create, mould or dig and plant in the earth for a living will choose to do so during their leisure hours.

Today with fast disappearing space and countryside, it is important that our nurseries present these materials to young children in order for them to have a period during this impressionable stage when they may explore substances that do not have the limitations of being man-made. Such materials will withstand all types of treatment and be completely consistent in their response — water and dry sand will pour through a sieve, wet sand can be moulded into shapes and clay will become slippery when water is added to it. In a world of inconsistent people it is reassuring and educative for a child to work with materials that have a sameness about them. With the exception of wood all these materials can be classed as 'messy'. The small neat modern home of today is not geared towards a roomy sandpit, a mud hole or room indoors where a child may freely use clay or water, and yet there is an instinctive need in a young child to get dirty and to use 'dirty' products. Often the nursery will be the only place where mess is tolerated without strain and where a child is enabled to come to terms with his own needs and later to use these materials in a truly creative way. We will look at each of these materials in turn to see their particular possibilities for play and ways in which they can be presented.

Water
Young babies enjoy water from the earliest age. Before birth the foetus is immersed in liquid in the womb and it has been suggested that this is why there is such an inherent fascination with the substance. It does have therapeutic value: timid and overanxious children gain confidence from its constant properties, hyper-active and aggressive individuals may be encouraged to make peaceful social contacts around a water tray, and warm baths are the ideal way to soothe a very disturbed or upset child. Apart from this, play with water inevitably provides a learning situation for the child as he discovers its sensory properties and later sees what it is capable of doing. It is important that these initial discoveries are not forced upon the child by the adult – the discovery must be made by the child and in his own good time for it to have the full impact: after that comes the value of adult intervention helping the child to link his discoveries and to draw further conclusions. Above all water should be presented in as many varied and attractive ways as possible with the emphasis on enjoying the play as this is the best way of encouraging further motivation.

Water is cheap and easily available and there should be no problem with provision. Basic equipment for play should include a deep, transparent water tray (or preferably two for syphoning purposes) to accommodate four or five children; waterproof aprons for the children and possibly wellington boots for the real enthusiast; heavy duty polythene if the floor is to be protected, with some old towels on the polythene to absorb surplus liquid; finally a roomy container or trolley which is divided into sections to hold different types of waterplay equipment.

The flexible teacher will seize upon any situations which involve water to allow the child time for experiment and discovery. For convenience we will look at some of the contrived and natural activities in which learning about water can develop indoors, outside and during wet wether. A detailed list of these activities will be found in Appendix C.

As with most activities for young children, indoor water play should not always be presented 'ready' for the children. They will derive enjoyment and gain a great deal if they help to fill the water tray (sometimes by bucket and sometimes by means of a hose), set out the protective covering and help clear up spills during the activity. Water can be presented cold, warm, with bubbles or coloured. By means of home-made and commercial equipment the children will discover how water moves, and what contains it. They will experiment with jugs, funnels and sieves, and reinforce their discovery that water falls through holes by repeating the activity again and again. They will enjoy blowing bubbles with pipes and metal loops and this is often an absorbing activity for the new or tearful child who in fact has no time to cry if he is busy producing bubbles. The child's toilet activities during the day will also give rise to discovery about water. When flushing the lavatory he could be shown the working of the cistern, and after washing his hands and pulling the plug out of the washbasin he will discover that the water always drains out in a circular fashion and that the circular direction is always the same. Cleaning surfaces with water after messy activities provides the opportunity for finding out about dissolving dirt and absorption of water into cleaning cloths. Cookery allows the child to see how by adding water to substances we change their nature e.g. making tea and coffee and dissolving jellies. Washing up after cookery and scrubbing dirty vegetables are both occasions for using water for cleaning.

Water play out of doors in fine weather is the ideal time for providing water on a larger scale. Paddling pools and garden hoses will give hours of delight as the children immerse themselves, lie and jump in the water, squirt and pour it over themselves. Outside surfaces can be 'painted' with water, and on a hot day the small painter will turn around to see that his 'painting' has already disappeared. Watering plants and vegetables in the garden is all part of the lesson on caring for living things. Even better if the nursery garden is equipped with a small stream then continuous experiments may take place throughout the year such as searching for live creatures, damming projects and watching to see how the weather affects the level of the water.

Wet, snowy and frosty weather can be enjoyed and exploited for discovery. So long as the children are adequately clothed there is no reason why they should not be out in all weathers. Catching rain drops and splashing in puddles and floating tiny home-made boats in rivulets of water are all joyful occupations, and are denied to the child who has to remain in the playroom. The feel and taste of snow is something special, particularly for the first time, as is seeing how quickly ice will melt in warm hands.

Sand
Sand has long been recognized as a popular and satisfactory play material for children. A sandy beach is perhaps the highest prerequisite for a happy holiday with youngsters, and a good-sized sand pit is a must for every nursery with outside facilities. It is a useful

material, being acceptable to the more fastidious children who may reject play with water and mud. Wet sand will inspire the child to create as it is so adaptable, and the sheer joy of using dry silver sand will cause a child to tip and pour endlessly purely for the sensory experience. Sandplay, inside and out, is a very social activity: children coming new to the nursery will spend some time at the sand tray filling and tipping, making sand pies and playing alongside others, not creating, but finding out the capabilities of the material. With increased confidence and sociability sand play will develop enormously: planned ventures will take place constructing and building in the sandpit outside: sand will be taken from one area to another in buckets or trucks and for specific purposes. When the child reaches this stage of play, extra materials will be required, particularly space outside for building projects and play where water and sand can be freely mixed. At first however, the newcomer will need to become familiar with dry and wet sand in the sandpit and sand tray and the best way he can do this is by using his hands: equipment is almost an impediment to basic discovery as it will inhibit the child's sensory experiences. Sand play should be available in all weathers, and therefore should be provided both inside and out. We will discuss both types of provision in more detail below with a detailed list of sand activities given in Appendix C.

Two sand trays are required indoors for both wet and dry sand. These need to have a good surface area rather than depth, and if the trays are fitted with wooden lids they can be used as activity surfaces for the children at times when the sand is not in use. A dustpan and brush placed under the sand tray will encourage the children to clear up their 'spills', and two partitioned containers are required to hold the varying sand tools. Different equipment should be kept apart for wet and dry sand, and at first the trays should hold only a limited selection of tools. As the child grows more able and less random in selection he can be given a wider choice of tools. These containers of equipment should be kept underneath or by the side of the sand tray. A quantity of silver sand purchased from a seed merchants is most suitable for indoor sand play (approximately half a hundredweight is required for a sand tray).

The child needs first of all to discover dry sand with his hands. He wili poke, press and trickle it and bury his hands in the heap of sand. He will delight in the cold heavy feel of the sand and let the fine grains tickle his skin. Silver sand is a clean material and there need be only the one restriction of not throwing it. Rules are best kept to an absolute minimum for effectiveness, but dangerous behaviour must be promptly stopped in all children and is an important social rule for them to learn. Dry sand behaves in a similar way to water and may sometimes be presented as an alternative. Equipment can gradually be introduced to enable the children to tip and pour the sand and to sift the grains through various meshes of coarse and fine weave. A sieve of fine mesh is a good way of cleaning the sand of dust and dirt and, given two containers, the children will enjoy doing this. The introduction of a magnifying glass will enable the grains to be studied and then compared with grains of soil.

Silver sand wetted down provides a very different medium for use in that it can be moulded with the hands and will stay put. Again, plenty of opportunity should be given for exploration without tools: wet sand can be smoothed, heaped and formed into ridges and balls. Wet sand play will give rise to imaginative ventures with the addition of miniature vehicles (plastic to avoid rusting) and other small toys. These additions will encourage the child to make his own relief map from the sand.

The essence of sandplay out of doors is a spacious sandpit with a ridge around the top to stop too much wastage and a generous paved surround. Silver sand in large quantities is very expensive, and a quantity of washed builder's sand is adequate (if it is not washed it will stain the children's clothes). At some stage the children will want to transport the sand and an additional sand 'dump', which can be a small paved area some distance away, will add to the play. A protective cover for the sandpit can be made from wooden battens and wire netting: this prevents the sand being fouled by animals. Apart from conventional sand play with moulds and buckets and spades, elaborate imaginative ventures may be established amongst the older children such as walls and bridges. A nearby supply of water will add to this play and cement and chocolate factories may be established using all available small containers.

Mud

The neat, tidy gardens of today allow few children to find out exactly what earth is. A patch of ground in the nursery garden and provision of some stout long handled spades will provide the opportunity to dig. The sheer satisfaction of being able to dig without coming to the bottom of the container is an excellent emotional outlet for aggressive instincts. The addition of water to earth is perhaps the messiest of play for children, and mud play is an age old activity, both absorbing and soothing. Mud can be smeared and moulded, and left to dry: if different types of earth are available, children may discover that some soils, like clay, will hold water whereas sand will absorb it. The value of mud however, is essentially its messiness. It can be looked upon as a socially acceptable substitute for children who have difficulties and fears of their excreta.

Clay

This material is not visually attractive and demands handling to discover its capabilities. It is cold and damp to touch and some children may be initially repelled until they meet the challenge of prodding and pushing it to change its shape. Clay is a material which channels energies and aggressions: it is absorbing and hard work and children around a clay table will not usually talk very much, their energies are directed into the material. Throwing clay onto a table will only improve its texture: it is socially approved for Johnny to heave lumps of clay around but not for him to continually thump his neighbour. Natural potters' clay is the most satisfactory for this age group. We are not looking for a modelling material as the emphasis is not on the finished product, but on working with the material and discovering its properties. Particular attention should be paid to the storage of clay: it should be kept in a polythene bag tightly tied, and stored in a bin with a close fitting lid. When it becomes too dry it should be moulded into small balls, a hole pushed into the centre and filled with water, and the clay should then be drawn over to hold the water. If it is then stored in the bin overnight, it should return to a reasonable consistency; this should allow the child to mould it without too much difficulty, and it should hold its shape.

Initially clay should be given to the child without tools, and plenty of time allowed for a large lump of clay to be 'discovered'. Harder lumps of clay can then be presented with a bowl of water and the child will be enabled to change the substance from something unmalleable to an oozing semi-liquid. After a time simple equipment will enable further investigation and stimulate ideas for using the clay. After initial exploration, the child will start to make balls and long coils from the clay: blunt knives should be offered for cutting, and clean lolly sticks and cut-off pieces of broom handle will allow him to tunnel through the clay, whilst wooden hammers will help him to bang his clay into shape. The opportunity to 'get to know' clay as a material is the most important stage at pre-school level: it is the 'using' and the 'doing' that is the delight. As the child approaches five years, or that stage of development, he will become capable of conceiving an idea and working to put it into practice. At this stage he announces that he wishes to make a snail and how does he make the horns? It is important to keep the simplest of pictorial reference books handy to meet these needs (even better of course to find a snail in the garden and to examine it under the magnifying glass) this is infinitely more valuable than the adult taking over and producing the snail herself.

By the time that the youngster is capable of making something vaguely representational and labelling it he may well wish to take it home, and this should be allowed even if the clay-bin empties rather sooner than anticipated. It is important to realize though that this stage is only reached by the few more mature children in the nursery: it is not necessary to purchase a commercial kiln for firing the clay, although a hardening additive may be added to the clay if they want to keep the finished results.

Dough

Although not strictly a natural material, and more refined and restricted than clay, dough does have some similarities, and as such has been included in this section. We refer here to the home-made materials of flour and water, commercial 'playdough' is both expensive, restrictive and messy to use. Home-made dough is very similar to pastry and is ideal for making 'pretend' cakes for use in the home corner. It is a more yielding material than clay and as such is not so suitable for aggressive outlets; often it provides a soothing and reassuring activity for newcomers to the nursery. Exploration and play with dough does not require the same absorption and fierce effort as clay, and because of this, conversation will tend to flow more freely around a dough table.

Sufficient dough for four children can be made from three pounds of plain flour, one and a half pints of water, half a pound of salt and a few drops of cooking oil. This can be coloured in delicate pastel shades with food colouring, or in more vivid tones with non-toxic powder paint. This particular dough retains its shape very well. A more elastic dough can be made by making up the mixture with self-raising flour and salt, and a 'growing' dough is obtained by adding yeast to the plain flour. The yeast mixture will only keep for a day or two: other dough can be kept for up to two weeks if stored in a polythene container with a tight fitting lid.

As with other materials, dough should first be presented to the child without tools to allow time for sensory discovery. After this, depending on the type of dough used, it can be a means of 'pretend' cooking, of making shapes and revealing prints, and can form a good base for stabiles (a more detailed account of presentation is given in Appendix C).

Wood

The abundance of cheap, easily broken plastic toys on the market today and the fact that wood is so expensive means that very few children have the opportunity of experiencing satisfactory play with durable wooden playthings at home. Because it is so strong it is used widely for equipment and for small toys and blocks in the nursery: here we will look at it as used on the woodwork bench. Carpentry is too sophisticated a word for the activity that takes place with three and four-year-olds. Again, the action and exploration is the crucial factor, but in this case, although the nature of wood will be explored with the hands, in order for the child to make any impact on it he must use tools. This activity is not a dangerous one if the teacher demonstrates simply how these tools are to be used; in this case it is necessary to show the child a technique in order for him to use the tool safely and with the maximum effect.

A regular supply of wood may be obtained cheaply or free of charge from a timber yard. The more irregular shapes there are the more potential interest is provided for the child, and although in the main the supply should be of soft wood, the occasional piece of mahogany will allow the child to learn that nails will not go easily into all wood. Manageable pieces of branches from various trees and fir cones will add to his experience of different woods. A selection of 'junk' such as milk tops, metal beer caps, corks and thick pieces of polystyrene will allow the woodwork to be extended to children who are not able to cope with nails and wood, but enjoy the action of hammering.

The woodwork bench should be the right height for a young child and should be solid and allow sufficient space for four children to work around it. If possible there should be provision for woodwork both indoors and out, and both woodwork benches should be equipped with two vices. A supply of good quality tools is important; toy tools are useless and a waste of money. A selection of small hammers, pincers, hacksaws, short handled screwdrivers and a hand drill should be provided. A selection of screws and nails can be kept in a tin with various compartments, and a magnet kept for clearing up spills.

Initially children will enjoy just hammering, and a large segment of tree-trunk will provide a good base for nails. Next, pieces of wood, hammers, nails, saws, glue and sandpaper need to be added. Sawdust can be collected from sanding pieces of rough wood. Screws, screwdrivers and a drill need to be kept for the more competent children who may express a wish to 'make' an object. These first creations are usually aeroplanes or swords and guns, and will involve nailing two pieces of wood together: the children may wish to paint their work and the powder paint in the painting area will be sufficient at this stage.

All these natural materials satisfy the most basic desires in children: they provide reassurance, calm aggressions and soothe anxiety and any guilt feelings that the young individual may have about his own body, about creating a mess and consequent pleasure derived from it. Such play nearly always takes place in a group around a table or container, and working with these materials encourages interaction with others.

Painting, drawing and sticking
This next set of activities aids the child to experience the sensory delights of colours, textures and shapes, and then, as his development progresses, he is able to order these experiences to some degree: his

drawings may assume the beginnings of representation, his paintings will no longer be random splotches of colour and his models may start to be 'something' – his discovery and investigation have given way to creativity. Because these media are instrumental for creative work, they are also expressive. A child of three and four is still limited in his language ability, particularly when his feelings are most intense, but he does need to make these feelings known, if only to give them some form for his own sake – painting and drawing are particularly expressive activities : sticking and cutting activities have been included here, because although they provide excellent manipulative practice, they are also expressive of a child's desire for form, shape and pattern in his life.

Painting and drawing
According to Kenneth Jameson in his book on *Pre-School and Infant Art* (1968) these two types of activity develop alongside one another in the young child. Very broadly a child begins to paint directly he comes into contact with the media – his initial efforts may be pure experimentation in putting brush to paper and experiencing the effect of colour : page after page may be filled with one colour whilst the child is absorbed with this process – later, one colour may be placed on top of the other, and later still the patches of colour start to be organized and placed side by side.

Whilst the painting activity can only take place with paint, drawing is possible for the child with any materials that make linear marks – this may be pencil, crayon, paintbrush or even the finger in the sand or on the misted window pane. The first results will be scribbles, seemingly meaningless, but out of these scribbles develops an oval form which the child will eventually develop into a big head and then into a representation that we recognize as a figure. (For more detail see *Pre-School and Infant Art*.) The painting activity is where the pleasure of colour is being explored ; the drawing is the beginning of the child learning to use symbols and harnessing this ability to recount experiences that matter to him. The development of painting and drawing will eventually merge when the child starts to create pictures of combined linear figures and patches of colour. At this stage he may start to give names to his finished results – whether they are recognizable to the adult or not is immaterial, because they have assumed a particular significance for the child – these first pictures will probably be symbols of familiar figures – 'my mummy' or 'my house'.

Sometimes, the delight in the finished work is so great that the child will dash to tell the adult all about it – very often however, particularly in the earlier stages the very act of painting or drawing is in itself cathartic and the end result completely unimportant. For this reason it is wise not to press a child to name his picture : sometimes it is impossible for him to do this, particularly when his work represents a tangle of feelings that he may no longer have because they have been purged through his activity. The best that the teacher can do for the young child in this area of his play is to provide the right materials, allow his work to be judged by himself, and give him every opportunity to develop originality: the latter can only be achieved if he does something for and by himself. Trying to copy or having to keep within the confines of lines will only sap confidence if it is not done correctly. Freedom to work as he wishes is perhaps the most important prerequisite for the child.

When looking at basic equipment for painting we should consider protective covering. The floor of a purpose built nursery unit should not need covering, but where protection is necessary, a good quality heavy polythene sheet is sufficient. The children will need smocks or aprons, and these may be commercial ones of rubber or plastic, or simply men's shirts suitably adapted at the neck and sleeves. These aprons should be hung on low hooks so that they are easily accessible to the children.

Painting easels are essential for ease of painting and for the child to see his marks developing as he is working. Other surfaces may be used however, such as covered walls, inside and out, paper on the floor or on tables. Brushes can be hogshair or nylon, which is more expensive but will give longer use, and brush sizes should be ten and twelve for this age group. Distemper brushes and paint rollers are excellent for the children to apply paint on large surfaces.

A variety of paper of different sizes, shapes, textures and quality should be offered for painting. These will include newspaper (mainly without pictures), white wrapping paper, lining paper and sugar paper. A selection of paper can be laid out on a low shelf or in a box in order for the child to choose for himself.

When purchasing paint, the large tins of powder paint are most economical and suitable for varied use. The youngest of children will only require limited primary colours, but soon a wide range of colours can be offered for the child to select for himself. Paint should be mixed so that the colour is strong and clear and not too runny in consistency. The short wax crayons provide large patches of colour quickly and are easy for small fingers to hold. Coloured pencils break quickly and are too rigid a media to be suitable, whereas felt-tip pens and spirit markers are expensive but colourful and effective to use. More specific drawing media are pencils and charcoal. Thick pencils with very soft lead are best for this age group, charcoal is messy to use, but the children will enjoy its bold results and will drag it sideways across the paper for smudgy results. Charcoal will also break easily, and should be offered in short thick pieces. When considering joint drawing areas, a marker board surface on the wall of the playroom with soft markerboard crayons which have an oily texture will be enjoyed, and ordinary coloured chalks are good for a large blackboard area. Children do find it fascinating to be able to obliterate their chalk pictures by wiping them off the board: this feeling of power is also manifested in painting when the representational picture is hurriedly covered over with thick paint. All the drawing media have certain advantages and add variety to the child's experimentation: however, just because some of them are tidy and non-messy materials, they should not be regarded as satisfactory substitutes for paint. The colour, texture and messy quality of paint are its real value.

The chance for the young child to experiment with paint and drawing media is so important that daily opportunities should be provided for this in the nursery. We have already seen that easel painting is perhaps the most convenient and practical for the young child, but he should have access to other surfaces on occasion, such as floor or wall painting. He should also be offered alternatives to paper as a surface: pieces of cardboard, cardboard cartons, wood and stone as surfaces will give rise to questions about porous qualities and comparisons can be made. Near the painting area a selection of drawing media can be made available to the child, and a table can be kept free to be used whenever required. It should be emphasized that painting and drawing essentially allow the child to experiment and to enjoy the experience and to develop the means of using symbols to recount these experiences. If all this is to happen then these materials must be used freely and filling in shapes, copying and using templates will only be inhibiting.

However, the child does need variety and we will discuss some painting 'techniques' that can be provided: they are not intended for the child to follow slavishly, but are rather regarded as extensions of the painting activity which may be suggested and the child encouraged to use the technique to further his own ends: in this way it will increase his experimentation rather than restrict it. (A more detailed list of painting techniques is given in Appendix C.)

A natural extension to painting with a brush is to paint with hands. Finger painting is messy and absorbing, and Kenneth Jameson describes it as 'Playing with Paint'. Recipes for finger painting include a cold water paste mixed to the consistency of cream, a maize starch mixed to a similar consistency and then added to whipped soap flakes, and a white sauce cooked as for eating and then left to cool. Powder paint may be previously added to the recipe, or a 'dollop' of cream may be placed on a formica topped table with one or two pots of powder colour placed by the side for the child to add as he wishes. The child will delight in the tactile experience of using the paint with his fingers and the beautiful swirling effects he obtains on the surfaces by twirling his finger tips. The activity of manipulating the paint is of the greatest importance, but after the child has had plenty of this experience he may be shown how to take a print from his pattern: if he places a piece of white paper face downwards onto the pattern, and after pressing firmly then removes the paper he will be delighted at this new way of 'making a picture'.

Printing will also provide for almost unlimited exploration by allowing the child to see what marks different objects make on paper. He may print with his hands or feet or use any printable object around him in the nursery (see Appendix C). Paint may also be used over waxed surfaces and can be blown through straws onto paper. It can be thickly and boldly smeared onto a surface with wooden spoons and palette knives or finely dabbed on with pipe cleaners and cocktail sticks. At first it is important that powder paint is mixed to a medium thick consistency for the child to avoid frustrations of it running down the paper or of being too thick to be workable. Later however, the child should be allowed to learn to mix his own paint and to see what different effects are gained by different consistencies. To encourage further experiment, emulsion paint, and powder paint mixed with different substances can be offered: sawdust and sand added to paint produce different results.

Sticking, cutting and tearing
Collage is an elaborate term for sticking: at a later stage in a child's career it might involve creating tasteful pictures (often representational) from a selection of materials. The child of three and four enjoys and benefits from a collage activity but mainly again on an experimental basis: materials must be explored, adhesives applied to see what will stick paper and what plastic. The basic knowledge that it is glue that does the sticking has to be realized: often a child will press two surfaces together with the glued side uppermost, or paint will be expected to act as an adhesive. Only after these investigations have been satisfied with the resulting delight that he (the child) may be instrumental in making one thing stick to another, will decisions about what is to be stuck and how, start to be made. At this stage the activity ceases to be random. Most pre-school activity is concerned with the action, then follows a change of emphasis when the child becomes capable of developing an idea and carrying it through. His development is such that he is able to conceive of a project in advance and then have sufficiently developed powers of concentration to use materials and start to create a recognizable likeness of an object. This is when the end product does matter and this stage is attained by a few older pre-schoolers. The value of the activity to most of the children will be exploration, to develop sensory experience by coming into contact with and using

rich colours and textures, to stimulate independent use of materials by enabling the child to select or to reject materials and to provide opportunities for him to destroy or take apart materials by tearing and cutting and to reshape or create new forms. It may be argued that the deprived or understimulated child will have stunted creative powers. If this is so it is usually because there has been no opportunity for him to use and explore relevant materials in his home environment – it is all the more important therefore for the child to be allowed this initial time when he appears to merely dabble and make a mess – out of this will grow the power of the imagination and confidence to create original works.

Collage may be two or three dimensional – that is sticking materials on paper or card, or using boxes and other waste materials. When providing for two dimensional collage, it is important that the paper or card is strong, that the adhesive is suitable and where necessary a variety of materials for sticking are attractively presented in containers. Adhesives may include a strong PVC glue such as Marvin Medium, masking tape or sellotape cut in 7cm (3″) strips and stuck around a saucer for easy use, vegetable glue or polycell for most paper work. Collage may also be set into a solid substance such as plasticine or polyfilla – here materials such as buttons or seeds are pressed in, at first in an haphazard way and later in increasingly elaborate patterns.

The range of materials suitable for sticking is also very wide. Natural sources are rich in variety: whilst on outings, children can collect seeds, nuts, shells, stones and feathers and their own collection may then be turned into their own collage. Fabrics, cooking materials and small junk are also all suitable.

Finally, there is particular social value in large joint projects in sticking and painting for young children. Large pieces of paper on the floor or wall, with sufficient paint and rollers or brushes for three or four children to work together encourages true cooperation. Joint collages may be done in the same way, and occasionally a large junk construction may be made from cartons. The children will grow to respect each other's working patch, and later to discuss and plan what form their work will take.

In this section on imaginative and creative activities, the emphasis has been very much on the child finding out for himself. Copying and reproduction are discouraged: what must develop is through the child's play and according to what he assimilates from his environment and how he accommodates to it, how his understanding of the world develops and his part in it. All the materials mentioned are ones which will allow the child the most satisfying means of developing his imaginative and creative powers, of soothing his frustrations and anxieties and in some measure of developing his social relations (this aspect will also be dealt with in other sections on play).

PHYSICAL PLAY

Looking back at the chapter on the pattern of development, we can see that a tremendous amount of physical competence is being achieved during those nursery years. As with creative development, the pace cannot be forced, but we should remember that the more opportunities that the young child has of practising skills, of using equipment that will aid development of these skills, the more sound is his resulting physical growth and consequently the greater his confidence. It becomes even more important to provide opportunity for the development of gross motor skills in the nursery as many of our children live in buildings without gardens, are restricted in their play because of hazards of traffic, and generally suffer from crowded living and the consequent lack of chances to run freely or to make a loud noise. This aspect of development is often not fully appreciated by uninitiated adults, who regard such activity as no more than 'letting off steam'. Of course it is this as well, but gradually, through the use of suitable provisions the child will begin to use his surplus energy in a purposeful way and his increased abilities will lead to increased independence.

Most of the activities involving gross motor development will take place out of doors – whilst we will concentrate on outdoor provision it is important to be able to make some large physical apparatus available to the children indoors in bad weather.

Suggested play to aid gross motor development

a Throwing and catching – provision of large and small balls, bean bags and rubber hoops.

b Running, skipping, jumping and hopping are all activities requiring space, and preferably a large grassed area – this will soften falls and enable the children to run barefoot.

c Climbing – a low branched tree is the natural and best provision, but sadly most nursery units must make do with substitutes. Rope ladders, steps, scrambling nets, climbing frames, thick ropes with knots for footholds, and steep hillocks in the garden will provide the child with plenty of opportunity to practise.

d Pulling and pushing – loading a truck with sand or earth and pulling it – pushing wheelbarrows – winding up pulleys.

e Use of wheeled toys to promote muscular development in the feet and legs and to teach the ability to steer – a selection of these toys should be made available including scooters, tricycles, go-carts.

However, whilst they aid physical development, they will only promote individual play and are therefore socially of little value to the child.

f Digging – a vigorous activity that will be catered for by provision of a large sandpit and area of earth. Long handled spades and trowels should be provided.

g Lifting and building – this is mainly achieved by using bricks, ramps and planks. It is one of the most valuable of the physical activities as it incorporates imaginative and social play – as the child builds his construction may become a house or cave and a group of children will develop elaborate fantasy play around their building.

This activity can take place inside or out – a good flat area should be provided with a variety of materials on hand to extend building activity, e.g. a steering wheel, pieces of carpet and curtain, large wooden vehicles. A good number of bricks are needed for four-year-olds in order for them to build 'large' – their walls need to be constructed to be taller than themselves, and their dwellings need to be crawled into.

The child's imaginative and physical capabilities will be stretched by providing other materials for building – these could include large coffee tins filled with dry sand and painted, large cardboard boxes, plastic or wooden milk crates, rigid polythene storage trays and tea chests, disused car tyres.

h Balance – a child will learn to balance by using building materials – at first he will build upwards, carefully constructing his tower until it crashes to the ground, which again provides its own delights – he then builds outwards and then the constructions start to become projects for a road or wall. Again, the greater the variety of bricks provided, the more the child will learn about balance. He needs to learn to balance his own body also, and the use of balance boards will develop this skill, or home made stilts constructed from large paint tins.

Physical development is a continuous process and will unfold to provide sound foundations in favourable conditions. The nursery garden should be particularly geared to provide these conditions and children should be allowed free access throughout the session. An adult should always supervise the outdoor area as accidents will occur. However, if the equipment provided is specifically geared to the needs of the under-fives, and the adult allows the child to set his own pace in acquiring skills, these accidents will be rare.

Suggested play to aid fine motor development
Hand–Eye coordination will develop by practice in:

a Threading – large wooden beads, square and round, on laces that, have one end stiffened. Milk tops, straws and buttons may be threaded with the aid of large darning needles and wool. Ribbons may be threaded in and out of loosely woven material.

b Sewing – sewing cards may be made by punching old greeting cards.

c Weaving – paper weaving from strips of coloured wallpaper interlaced on a sheet of dark paper.

d Carving – large block of washing soap or a block of salt can be carved with blunt knives.

e Tipping and pouring with dry sand or water.

f Social skills of self-dressing and feeding – as with other activities, time should be allowed for the child to 'do it himself'. It would seem more practical for the child to learn these skills naturally during the course of the day when dressing to go out or at meal times, rather than in a more artificial situation when using lacing and buttoning boards.

g Commercial manipulative toys e.g. small table bricks, jigsaw puzzles, lego etc. These are useful extras to have in a nursery and a range of them should be freely available to the child. Most of this equipment tends to encourage solitary play and is consequently often good introductory material for the newcomer. Because of its solitary nature however, and the fact that many children are already provided with similar materials at home manipulative toys should never take the place of the more open ended media in the playroom.

h Painting, cutting, tearing, sticking and drawing – all these activities mentioned in the creative section serve an important function in strengthening wrist and finger manipulation and control and good experience with these media are a necessary prerequisite for the child's later ability in letter formation.

i Finger rhymes will encourage dexterity.

Whereas adult intervention and participation is advocated in many aspects of nursery play, physical play provision requires the adult only to see that no accidents occur and to give active encouragement to a child who is gaining a skill – the most important requirement is for the adult to see that the right circumstances for physical development are present, and, given these the child will use the environment to develop the more efficient use of his own body. Lady Allen of Hurtwood says:

It is too often forgotten that small children, like older children of school age, need a place where they can develop self-reliance, where they can test their limbs and senses and their brain, so that brain, limbs and senses gradually become independent of their will.

To look upon our nursery provision as such a testing ground means that we must examine provision in the playroom and garden very carefully.

COGNITIVE PLAY

The three previous aspects of development, that is the social, emotional and physical growth of the child, and activities suggested to enhance this growth give little occasion for controversy – nearly all parties concerned with early childhood will agree that the types of equipment and stimulus so far suggested are suitable and adequate. The argument arises when we consider how much time and emphasis should be given to promoting a child's intellectual growth in a planned nursery environment. We have so far suggested that a child's growth is interrelated – by looking at his early development we have seen that many things are happening simultaneously and when a child plays he is adding to and reinforcing different experiences which aid his maturity. Yet many experts, Bereiter and Englemann for example, would say that we are not necessarily providing the most suitable environment, particularly for culturally deprived children, if we concentrate on planning for a child's all round growth. They would argue that a child's cognitive growth comes before all else if the effects of cultural deprivation are to be overcome and they would provide an environment which aids cognitive acquisition to the detriment of other development which they suggest will follow naturally as the individual achieves academic success. Maya Pines (1967) describes the controversy which rages between the group of child development specialists who believe in educating the total child from the experience around him, which he will absorb if he is in a sufficiently enriched environment, and the cognitive psychologists who argue that because motivation is so strong during these early years we should be making the most of it by extending learning situations, closely interacting with the child and developing his cognitive abilities in a much more specific way. This argument is still continuing and the pendulum appears to be swinging towards providing a more structured environment, particularly in providing selective programmes for language development for our children from disadvantaged backgrounds.

What approach does this book promulgate? We fall very much between two stools believing that there is much to be said for both arguments. We accept that learning is sequential and any premature attempt to push one particular facet of development forward will prevent sound growth. We also accept that unless a child has foundations to enable him to start controlling his angers and fears, to aid him to build relationships with others, and to have mastery over his body, his ability with symbols and other abstract learning will be relatively meaningless. However it is indisputable that the cognitive aspect of a child's development is important, particularly when the child comes from a home lacking in language stimulus or any attempt to help him understand his world. This is also the one aspect of early childhood education that has been glossed over in the past. The rather hazy idea that the child will, by a process of osmosis, learn what he requires by interacting with his peers in a stimulating environment whilst the adult stands by to replenish paper on painting easels and see that aprons are put on for water play, is one that is held in many pre-school institutions today. This is unfortunate because the beginnings are right – a rich environment and the opportunity to socialize are necessary – but the child will require specialized help first of all to make sense of his environment and then to aid and develop his powers of inquiry by having his explorations guided and at least some of his findings pinpointed. Situations do need to be set up to ensure that the child does make discoveries and the discovery needs to be made by him in order for it to be exciting and to have impact: however many of these discoveries will be random and unconnected and the teacher needs to come in here to help the child process what has been discovered and start to form links in his chains of thought. Much of this teacher-child interaction will be required in fostering language skills and this is dealt with in the next section. The teacher will also need to look carefully at the nursery environment, making sure that the activities and apparatus provided do interest the children and that there are sufficient new experiences throughout the term to provide novelty without overwhelming the child. Finally, the teacher needs to observe the child making his discoveries in order to find out what stage of cognition he has reached and what should be presented next. It is not necessary or at all desirable for this cognitive development to take precedence over other activities: the nursery day should proceed in its free, varied way whilst the teacher moves from one small group to another or occasionally works with an individual to discuss material, learn facts and further more investigation.

We will discuss three areas in which the teacher can best aid the child to acquire concepts: these are providing sensory experience in the nursery, setting herself and other adults up as models for imitation and helping the child to gain the equipment to learn, that is motivation and language acquisition.

Our nursery child is at the pre-operational stage of development as described by Piaget. He starts to play symbolically and to explore his world in a more able way than the random exploration of the baby.

He has gained sufficient control over his body to move freely in his environment, he has started to socialize and to interact with others and their explorations add to his own : because of his developing language his actions during the day are being internalized and fused into thought processes. We have seen that this internalization of thought can start to take place whilst the child is still at the sensori-motor stage when he starts to anticipate events and to build up picture images in his mind. However the process is greatly accelerated when these pictures can be formulated into words : often one sees a three-year-old talking quite openly to himself whilst he is absorbed in activity, and the talk is directed at what he is doing. Here he is formulating his activity into simple language that he understands, so that what are now word images of his actions may be stored away into his ever expanding frames of reference.

Only when the child's activity becomes meaningful to him will he use his language to aid him to internalize it. The process whereby the phenomenon becomes meaningful however must first be through direct contact. A three-year-old will only have had a minute amount of experience during his lifetime, most of the situations, particularly those planned for him in the nursery are novel ones and he needs to become familiar with them. His powers of thought are still at a primitive stage and his means of learning are through his sense organs which have also developed since his sensori-motor period. He will need to look, listen, feel, taste and smell his environment, and to repeat this involvement again and again until different experiences make sense and are internalized, and the teacher will observe by the child's reaction that he is ready to move on to the next stage of learning. The setting up of a variety of sensory stimulus in the nursery then is a prerequisite for the child's intellectual growth, and some suggestions for such stimulus are now given.

Visual

A young child does react immediately to things he sees. He will rush up eagerly to any new piece of equipment or activity in the playroom that morning, or wander away from his mother if his eye catches the toyshop window. It is important that we recognize his visual receptiveness and also make an attempt to understand that many things a child is looking at he is seeing for the first time, and certainly never with an adult's experience. This 'fresh eye' to the world and the enthusiasm that goes with it should be exploited whenever possible. The impact of a nursery on any newcomer should be visually exciting. Brightly coloured curtains and pictures on the walls, coloured equipment and interesting designs of wallpaper in the home corner, gay tablecloths and flowers at dinnertimes all help to provide a pleasing situation for young children. Apart from providing the setting the teacher will use every means to extend her children's visual curiosity. She may work on projects to develop the child's sense of colour. Colour displays will help this. A table with a widely varying selection of different shades of red will start the child on the road to knowing what red is about. These displays however will lose half of their value if they are beautifully arranged beforehand by the teacher – the children need to play an active part searching and contributing to the selection. The children may also look through different colours by providing home-made spectacles with lenses of different coloured cellophane or covering part of the window with coloured cellophane.

Collage tables presenting a rich variety of one colour materials will reinforce colour concepts e.g. a selection of red crepe paper, wool, tissue, fur and buttons.

Painting will provide the delight of placing brilliant colour onto paper, and later the ability to experiment with mixing colours and seeing results.

Colour matching will precede the naming of colours and practice can be given with sorting and matching games.

In the garden tracks of stones or shells may be laid for the children to follow and find 'treasure'. The outside should provide constantly changing visual experience with the seasons, a flower garden and wealth of small wild life – a few small magnifying glasses outside will give the discovery of insects even greater visual impact.

We should remember that whenever possible the children should be given real objects to look at rather than representations – it is impossible to expect that a small child should have gained any concept of an elephant by looking at a picture or even by seeing a television programme: the immense size, texture of skin and 'live' quality are totally lost. First hand experience will provide the breadth of concept, and displays of pictures should be mainly the children's own work. They can help arrange it at their eye level, and arrangements should be changed frequently.

Auditory

Our children are born into a world of constant noise. Traffic, machinery and mass media contribute to make the early years spent in the home noisy ones. Young children also like to make noise. Margaret Lowenfield suggests that exercise of the body, of the voice, of the whole person in production of the maximum possible commotion is an absolute necessity at some time or other to every healthy child. 'Noise is necessary, movement is necessary, and to be healthy these must be allowed to be exactly what they are – shapeless explosions of overplus of energy.' We should make provision for this need in our tolerance towards noise and activity and by having suitable physical outlets to hand.

The fact that a child has generally been so used to living with a confusion of noises does tend to dull his auditory sense. Most children today also watch a great deal of television, and are therefore more used to visual rather than auditory impact. The child's ear needs to be fully aroused in the nursery if he is going to be made aware of the wealth of different sounds with which he is living. Children need to develop the art of listening, a receptive skill, in order to develop their speech which is expressive, and they need to be able to distinguish letter and word sounds before starting to read. A knowledge and interest in sounds will lead to an appreciation of music. This listening can be encouraged by discovery situations for the children to explore for themselves and through the teacher's interaction with small groups of children.

The following suggestions are to help develop auditory discrimination:

a Sound tables may be set up displaying a variety of materials to be tested for sound effects – a selection of bells, of ticking clocks, of articles to be tapped or banged, or milk bottles filled with different levels of liquid.

b Shakers may be made by filling plastic containers with different materials e.g. peas, lentils, dry sand. After the children have helped to make the containers, they should be encouraged to use them and to decide what materials make what sounds.

c Very simple patterns of sounds, e.g. clapping, can be given to small groups who should then be encouraged to repeat the pattern themselves.

d Practice in listening to the direction of sounds: a child may be encouraged to close his eyes and guess from which direction of the room a sound is being made.

e Short recorded radio programmes (particularly designed for the under-fives) and records (see appendix D) are suitable for small group listening.

f Recordings of different sounds e.g. birdsong, rain falling, wind, trains, aeroplanes may be given and the children asked to identify particular sounds.

g Story and music sessions will encourage the child to listen (see pp 116–200.

Tactile
Young children react intuitively to touch: they need physical contact

and will crowd around at story time, clutching the teacher's knee and placing an arm around her neck. They will stroke her stockinged leg or finger her fur collar, their fingers seeking and exploring. This searching for physical reassurance becomes greater as the child becomes tired and vulnerable at the end of the day.

A child also needs to have plenty of physical contact with the basic materials of the world around him, and, as we have discussed, their initial explorations with these materials are sensory (see pp 81–93).

Again modern living has deprived many children of tactile experiences. New houses have smooth plastered interiors, furniture is vinyl and plastic, pavements and roads are uniform in texture and the majority of childrens' toys today are designed from smooth plastic. The nursery will aim to balance this by providing a wide variety of textures and allowing the child to explore them freely: the teacher will help him to verbalize his discoveries. The following suggestions will provide some tactile experiences for young children:

a The nursery playroom can have walls decorated with different textures e.g. cork, hessian. Garden paths outside can include different surfaces, e.g. cobbles, crazy-paving or cinders.

b 'Feeling' tables can be set up where the children may help to find and arrange a variety of different fabrics or a selection of prickly and smooth or hard and soft articles.

c 'Feeling' bags where articles of a provocative shape may be hidden and later identified by the child feeling them.

d Collage activities will encourage exploration using materials of varying textures e.g. a selection of pasta, fabrics, corrugated paper, feathers.

e Dressing up promotes tactile experiences with silky scarves, furry hats and velvet cloaks and other luxurious items.

f Allowing the child to go barefoot will provide great satisfactions: the teacher can talk to him about why he loves the feeling of running on grass or why he creeps slowly and carefully on loose pebbles.

g Children's collages and paintings can be displayed at their level to encourage them to be felt as well as seen.

Tasting

Some of the children entering the nursery are still at the oral stage of development when everything is tested by being placed in the mouth. As the child develops he tends not to put such great emphasis on oral experience as other means of testing his environment are now open to him.

There are areas for encouraging development of taste, and also preaching caution. A young child is naturally conservative in his taste in food: he is unlikely to be immediately enthusiastic about any new food introduced at dinner time and may well need gentle persuasion to attempt it. He should be encouraged to try different foods in tiny portions, but firm likes and dislikes should be respected. On the other hand, a child's natural curiosity may lead him to taste any interesting plants or berries in the garden. Whilst one hopes that the nursery garden would never contain anything poisonous it is as well to suggest firmly that a child should never sample anything strange without asking an adult.

Taste tables arranged with a variety of substances in small pots for the children to taste (with approval) may be approached reluctantly by all but the more adventurous individuals. Their perception of taste may be sharpened by these experiences and they should be encouraged to describe the different tastes.

Olfactory

A child's sense of smell may be developed by the teacher commenting on the strong scent of the hyacinths in the room or the delicious smell emanating from the kitchen where the chocolate cakes are cooking. He will surely have been surrounded by these experiences before, but his senses need training to detect them. A 'smelling' table with several strong smelling substances e.g. talcum powder, orange peel, onion will encourage discrimination and comment.

Using sensory experiences

If the child is given a full range of sensory stimulus, together with an adult's help to enable him to make use of the stimulus, he is likely to be accumulating a fund of experience which he must be helped to organize if it is going to aid his cognitive skills. His sensory play with natural materials will develop as he starts to perceive cause and effect; concepts of capacity and volume will start to emerge from his waterplay activity; he will perceive size and shape from repeatedly handling three dimensional objects at the junk sticking table. He will start to sort, classify and count after playing with the coloured buttons on the display table. The teacher will notice these developments from the way in which the child plays or from his comments. She will help clear up any confusion in his discoveries and provide him with correct terms and descriptions for his discoveries. John Holt (1971) states that:

True learning – learning that is permanent and useful, that leads to intelligent action and further learning – can only arise out of the experience, interests and concerns of the learner. Every child, without exception, has an innate and unquenchable drive to understand the world in which he lives and to gain freedom and competence in it.

This statement is doubly true of our youngest children whose urge to learn is unmarred and fresh. It is this precious quality that nursery teachers need to nurture and utilize because this is what each individual requires in order to learn throughout his life. During debates about what skills nursery environments should be fostering and what results primary teachers should be seeing the desire to learn must be regarded as the most important.

When looking at the driving curiosity of the three or four-year-old it is difficult to conceive that this motivation to learn will ever be dulled. The hungry urge to absorb a new situation; the ceaseless questions that first his mother is faced with, and then as he becomes familiar with the nursery situation his teacher must be prepared to answer: the flitting from one activity to another which is so characteristic of a new child in the nursery just because he needs to sample everything at once. All these are in some way typical of nursery children, but the more barren the child's environment, the more likely it is, that once having settled in, he will show this overwhelming eagerness to feed on rich new situations. The nursery teacher has no need to remind her children to 'get on with their work'. Three to five-year-olds will work ceaselessly, their play is synonymous with their work: they will gather eagerly around a new activity table, ask for stories, dig furiously in the garden gathering specimens for the nature table, and still look for more.

How then is this precious learning drive to be preserved and extended, and what features in a nursery may possible endanger it? It may well be that one of the differences between nursery and primary schooling and secondary schooling is the way in which motivation is dealt with. The teacher dealing with the younger child will do all she can to extend a learning drive: child-centred learning is essentially motivation emanating from the child as a result of him interacting with children and adults in a conducive environment (either at home or in school). This motivation is then nurtured by the mother, and then the teacher, providing more situations and additional materials for the child to use, and participating herself by discussing, questioning and expanding. During the early years in particular the teacher will mainly follow the child's direction of interest. As the child becomes older, he is expected to follow the teacher's direction of interest, until by the secondary stage of schooling the child is studying specific subjects, and all too soon the pressure is on for him to become competent in each of these subjects at an examinable level. Long before these examinations loom up, many of the children have lost their motivation to learn, lost the desire to attend school which is in their opinion, a place entirely irrelevant to their needs. John Holt puts it forcefully when he says: 'It is a rare child indeed who can come through his schooling with much left of his curiosity, his independence, or his sense of his own dignity, competence and worth.' It is not within the scope of this book to make recommendations to alter secondary curricula, but to emphasize the value to a learning situation for the nursery teacher to employ a child-centred approach. By all means stimulate, suggest, and bring in all manner of materials to act as starting points for learning, but let the child's interest set the pace. The nursery teacher who makes out a timetable of activities at the beginning of the week and can say at the end of that week that she has adhered to her timetable is a suspicious teacher indeed: children's needs and interests do not fit neatly into timetables. An initial framework is essential for every teacher to have when planning her day, but this framework must be as flexible as possible to allow for waxing and waning motivation.

If we are really going to be honest about having a child-centred approach in our nurseries then our activities must be voluntary. The compulsory story group attended by twenty-five three and four-year-olds daily may well establish a settled routine of getting the group together, it may well get the children used to sitting in a large group for ten or fifteen minutes daily, but it will not develop every child's desire to hear stories: there is the danger that it will encourage some children to sit quietly, and effectively 'switch off' each time that story period is introduced. In the same way a love of outdoor activities or of music will not be encouraged by insisting that every child goes into the nursery garden for at least some part of the session, or by having a mass music session, with everyone being jollied into joining in. If the children are encouraged to use indoor or outdoor premises at will: if it is understood by the children that music and story sessions are part of the daily routine and are held for anyone interested (the only rule being that once you attend, it is polite to stay until the end so as not to interrupt the rest of the group) then everyone gains, the teacher has a highly motivated group of children with whom to work, and the rest of the group are working with something else that is holding their interest at the time.

Finally, a child-centred approach to learning does mean keeping in tune with the child's direction of energy and not pulling him in the opposite direction. Tidying up, washing one's hands, dressing to go outside are all important and necessary activities during the day so *long as they are made relevant to the child*. If it is simply explained that unless he tidies up his materials he may be unable to find them the next day because the caretaker will have thrown them away, that unless he washes his hands before he eats he may carry germs to the meal table, that unless he dresses properly to go outside he may become ill and then not be able to come to school, the child may not at first accept these explanations, but in time these routines will become a meaningful part of his activity, and not distract from it. This will only happen if the teacher is also aware that these routine requirements should be brief and only undertaken when necessary; they are *not* time fillers and there is no excuse for seeing long periods of tidying up undertaken several times a day, or queues of children waiting to go to the washbasins or waiting to get dressed to go outside.

Our last requirement for concept development is the acquisition of language. In our concern whether to present a nursery environment as simply an enjoyable experience for small children, or a training ground for future life, one aspect of the child's development is being seen as increasingly important, and this is his ability to be able to communicate verbally. Bernstein draws the important distinction between the simple and elaborated code of language as employed by working and middle-class families. Dr Joan Tough follows this by emphasizing how important it is to consider the acquisition of language as a tool for learning. She describes the types of language needed: 'they are the skills of logical argument, of examining a range of possible solutions to problems, of anticipating and planning, and of framing questions which will bring the kind of information required. These are the tools of thinking.'

These experts and others state firmly that the means of communication leading to more efficient learning ideally take place first of all in the home. Where the parents actively involve the child in meaningful conversation leading to the types of language outlined by Dr Tough, then that child is equipped for a headstart in his schooling. Where the child has only been talked at in monosyllables, and has learned during his formative years that his attempts at speech are regarded as a noise or a nuisance, his development will be very different. His language growth may not have even been restricted unpleasantly, he may have loving parents, and may be living in a home where language is freely used, but conversation to him will be in the form of instructions and concern for his behaviour and no reinforcement will be given to his struggling verbal expressions. As with any learning, unless the child receives this essential reinforcement from babyhood onwards, when his babbling is forming into words and then eventually into sentences, he will not be motivated to further development. Such a background without this reinforcement will produce children who come into a pre-school environment finding it difficult to respond to any other form of language than the restricted code of their parents, and certainly unable to use words themselves in any elaborated way. This language deficiency may affect their total development: until they can express themselves in conversation full social contacts are not possible and emotional frustrations may arise – certainly their cognitive development will be stunted. (See pp 61–8 on Piaget)

Briefly then we can see how crucial satisfactory language development is to the young child, and although the nursery environment is not in existence solely to push skills into its individuals we do our children a real disservice if we do not aid them to acquire use of language in the same way as we assist their social, emotional and physical development. Just how should the nursery teacher set about doing this? She will look first to the child's experiences – gain what knowledge that she can of his home environment and see how his experience in the nursery balances and in some cases compensates for his home. She will attempt to ensure that all of her children have a great many first hand experiences of the activities outlined in our previous section. Bearing in mind the importance of young children learning through their senses, she will allow every opportunity for this in order for them to start internalizing their experiences and to develop understanding of what they are talking about. The nursery teacher will not, however, allow these experiences to take place in a vacuum – she will suggest, discuss, question and listen to the child, gently encouraging him to think about his experiences and to develop them. She will, particularly with the more deprived child, attempt to emulate the advantaged home environment where the business of life is discussed with the child. She will seize every opportunity during a nursery session to develop a child's awareness of a situation, and to see that he is formulating this into language.

So satisfactory language development for many children is dependent upon the teacher's active participation in their play – the days when it was sufficient to keep them well and happy are long past. However the experienced and aware teacher knows that there are times when she must stand apart: as with other aspects of growth she must look to the child and see what is required for the individual. It may well be that a child's language may be initially retarded or inhibited during the early days of settling into a nursery, or that a child is slow at making relationships and prefers to play in a solitary and silent fashion for some time – in these cases, patience and time are needed to see how the child progresses before tackling his language. The teacher also needs to be sensitive to the fact that there are very valuable times of growth for a child in the nursery when adult intervention is not needed – these times may be ones of intercourse with his peers, of wrestling with his emotions or of making some exciting discovery – but he needs to do this without adult aid. These are the times when the teacher will be observing and listening to give her a clue as to what has been learned, and what the next step of learning is to be.

There is at present controversy as to whether structured language programmes are required for our more deprived children. Many nursery teachers are frightened of the word 'structure', believing it to mean an end to the essential freedom and self-regulation of the nursery environment. It should be remembered however that structure is implied in any meaningful situation, by deliberate choice of materials and activities for the children. Research until now has led us to believe that there is no adequate substitute for real experience for the child — pictures and books are a good second best at this stage. Some children however may be so backward in speech that they will need a one to one relationship with a teacher daily in a secluded room where all attention may be focused on learning words through experience and using them meaningfully. The teacher may be helped by using a specific language kit for a child — if this gives her confidence then surely this can only assist the child. One important point however; in using any such kit, the teacher should never lose sight of the specific needs of her individual child — his needs cannot be adapted to the programme, and the programme therefore needs to be adapted to assist him.

6
Areas of discovery

It is arbitrary to select certain experiences for young children and label them discovery situations, as ideally the total environment, both at home and in the nursery, should provoke discovery. As we have seen a child is most certainly 'discovering' as part of his interaction with all the media so far mentioned: because of his limited experience he is likely to be confronted with new phenomena daily and these are stored away to take their place in his frame of reference, whether it is a realization that water falls through holes or that a brushful of paint on paper provides a splash of colour. This chapter discusses areas of activity that cannot be placed under one heading of social, emotional, physical or cognitive development. They may help boost all of this development (e.g. a cookery table is a reassuring activity for a child new from home, it is a sociable group experience, involves mathematical concepts of weighing, measuring and capacity, and the mixing involved provides good practice for fine motor control) but they are included here primarily because they challenge the child to investigate, and become more aware and more familiar with situations and things around him.

OUTSIDE THE NURSERY

Living things
As we have mentioned, a young child needs first hand experiences in order to achieve sound learning. However good a picture of a tree it cannot replace the real thing, it cannot convey the size of the tree trunk, the texture of the bark, the shape, design, colour and feel of the leaves. Any experience of nature must be concrete, and this is possible even in the tiniest of nursery gardens.

Children should be given some idea of how things grow. A life cycle of a seed which they have planted for themselves and seen growing, producing leaves, flowers, more seeds and then dying is surely a simple introduction to their own life cycle. Seeds need to grow quickly and easily as the children will be looking for quick results. A group of children can help to dig a small vegetable and flower plot in the spring time. Peas, carrots, lettuces, radishes and beans are all easily grown, and a packet of hardy annual flower seeds should produce some colourful results. If there is no space for growing in the garden there are still many possibilities inside. Mustard and cress can be grown on blotting paper, in egg shells of soil or scooped out potatoes filled with soil; apple and orange pips will eventually grow into tiny shrubs; grass seed grows quickly on damp cloth or shallow containers of soil; carrot or swede tops will sprout feathery leaves in a saucer of water; onions and other bulbs will grow if the bulb is balanced with its bottom not quite touching the water. Plants and bulbs can be dissected after flowering: just how do they grow? What do they need to grow? Does the shoot or the root grow first?

Moulds are often avoided by teachers because of unpleasant smells, but under a magnifying glass (a large one, preferably securely clamped to the table) many moulds look beautiful and the children will see them growing daily. Pieces of stale cheese, damp bread and milk all produce excellent results.

Young children have a great capacity for enjoying the present: they enthuse about their discoveries, but do not always appreciate the links or the full implications of what they find. This is often true of their attitude towards the changing seasons, and here it is for the teacher to help them to draw the threads together and become aware of the seasonal pattern. Spring is the time for digging in the garden, for discovering insects scuttling in the first sunshine and finding the first spring flowers: even the city children may bring samples of coltsfoot into the nursery, and if at all possible a small section of the nursery garden should be kept 'wild' to encourage weeds and wild flowers to be 'discovered' by the children. A small amount of frogspawn kept carefully will allow the children to see the fascinating development of the frog: so much better if the spawn can be collected from a pond by the children as then they can see the frog's natural habitat.

Warmer weather, the advent of paddling pools, more flowers in the garden and leaves on the trees give promise of the summer. This is perhaps the loveliest time for the children as so many activities can take place outside, clothing is simple and unrestrictive and the more fortunate group have experiences of seaside holidays. Shadow play can take place in the sunshine with the children becoming aware of how they can change the shape of their own shadows. Caterpillars may be kept so long as it is known what food they will eat, and if a buddleia bush is kept in the garden a selection of butterflies will be attracted to it.

Very soon after the children have returned to school after the summer holidays the morning chill in the air and the colouring of the leaves will tell of autumn. This season is a rich provider for the children. They can examine fine, dewy spider's webs seen on the grass early in the mornings: they may even be fortunate enough to see tiny mushrooms sprouting through the grass (caution must be shown in distinguishing which are mushrooms and which toadstools). Berries, nuts and seedheads can be collected in profusion, sorted, displayed and used for collages. The child should be told quite firmly that none of these items should be tasted without first asking an adult. Bulbs should be planted and placed in a dark shed ready for the spring. The children will enjoy planting them in moist bulb fibre and discussing the picture of the flowers, but by the time the bulbs are ready to bring out again they will have been quite forgotten.

The coming of winter means that many of the animals hibernate, the trees are losing the last of their leaves which make coloured crunchy carpets on the ground. Frost patterns may be noticed on the window panes; foggy mornings provoke interest, and the first fall of snow invites a mass exodus into the garden just to sample it. Tracks and footprints may be noticed easily in snow: snow may be taken indoors to see how quickly it will melt. Birds need to be fed and bird 'cakes' may be made from almost any scraps of food. A bird table is a great source of interest at this time of year.

These are just a few of the seasonal activities that will help the children to realize how the seasons alter and what happens during different times of the year. A simple nature table kept specifically for their findings with pictures and reference books to help extend the discoveries may be kept 'alive' with interest throughout the year. The table should be kept attractive and changed regularly, and the children encouraged to watch for any new additions, and search for any contributions that they can make to it.

It is becoming less and less common for children to keep animals in their home, and if a nursery has the space it can offer valuable experience to a child by having a small area for pets. Lessons need to be learned in caring for something totally dependent – how much does it eat and drink – what does it need for its bed and how does one clean its cage? If the animal has babies the children will become acquainted with the reproduction process and when it dies they will be able to see the lack of movement and the rigidity of the animal and start to understand something about the fact of death. It is important that the children are shown the correct way to handle the animals and for the pets to become used to being held for a limited time. A child will derive great sensory satisfaction from stroking the silky coat of a rabbit, from feeling its long ears and sharp claws, and seeing its sensitive whiskers. They will feel its strong hind legs and enjoy seeing it use them to hop. Such a story as *The Tale of Peter Rabbit* will be so much more meaningful after this real experience.

Rabbits and guinea pigs are the most suitable animals to keep outside in pens. Gerbils, hamsters, mice are all ideal to have in the playroom. Slow worms, newts and turtles are all possible to keep for a limited time. A few hardy goldfish in an attractive acquarium are probably the easiest of all pets to care for. A variety of these pets will allow the children to compare different needs and ways of life.

Outings

Children at the nursery will come with a wide variety of different experiences, and this will include their knowledge of the outside world. Some children today at three and four are quite familiar with airports and holidays abroad. Some may be in the happy situation of looking forward to a different weekly outing with their family, and others may come from families where there is no money for the extra luxuries of transport and the adults have no spare emotional energy to take their children to new situations and enjoy new experiences with them.

Outings are important for all young children as a means of widening their environment and making them aware of what other people do and what makes up their community. Outings planned from the nursery can appeal to children from all backgrounds. However wide his experience, a child often does not have the opportunity to go for a walk at his own pace, to have interminable questions answered and have many posed to him which will enable him to consider his findings even more carefully. Often he does not have the chance to share an outing with his peers: half the delights of discovery are in sharing. The child who is normally deprived of outings at home will benefit even more if the nursery trips are carefully planned as part of an enrichment policy for him.

It is not necessary to have ambitious nursery outings, in fact it is positively unwise to take small children on journeys of more than half an hour, to stay out for long periods, or attempt a tightly scheduled programme. It should always be remembered that some of the children have only recently settled into the nursery and made the break with mother. These children may now appear completely confident within the nursery but once outside in a new situation this confidence may well crumble. If a coach journey is undertaken it is a good idea to invite parents of younger children to accompany them. Good parent teacher relations may often be established on a happy informal occasion such as this.

Walks within the locality are ideal for young children, particularly if they are to see something specific. A walk to the local pillar box may be timed to see the postman open the box for letters: even better if one of the children posts a letter addressed to the nursery and the children can then see it delivered to the school the next morning.

Going to the shops is always popular, perhaps to visit the greengrocers to buy apples for the daily snack, or to the florist to choose seeds for the garden. A supermarket provides endless store of discussion, and sometimes it is possible to visit the back of the store and see goods being unloaded from the delivery vans and refrigerated lorries. Some schools will be fortunate to have a park nearby: parks and any country visits provide a good source of discoveries for the nature table. If each child is given a small paper bag in which to make his own collection, the discoveries of leaves, twigs, stones and other interesting objects will be more personal and the child should be allowed to decide what he wishes to do with them afterwards. Conservation of all living things should be discussed with the children, and only samples of the most abundant weeds should be collected. Even in the most barren of areas a walk will assume interest if the group of children are encouraged to look at what is growing in front gardens, compare the colours of front gates, or note the numbers on front doors.

Outings of particular interest may include a visit to a farm, a zoo, a fire station, a dock or a building site. These are the visits which require rather more careful planning with a ratio of one adult to every five children and some previous investigation to see if any of the children have any particular fears of animals or large machinery. As with most nursery activities, outings are best undertaken with small groups of children: this enables the visit to be more informal and on the lines of a family outing. Sometimes it is enough to take a small group for a ride on a bus, or even better a short train journey which is often a totally new experience these days for many children.

In order to achieve the maximum effect the proposed visit should be discussed first of all with the group, and possibly followed up with relevant music or stories e.g. a ride on a train could be followed up by a session discussing the movement of the train, a short record of engine sounds and the story of *The Little Red Engine* by Diana Ross, which remains a favourite despite steam engines being long out of fashion. Very often however, particularly with children who are unused to going out, a visit will appear to have little immediate effect and the teacher may be disappointed if she expects lots of lively discussion and representational paintings. A child might well take considerable time to bring this new piece of stimulus into his frame of reference and it may be weeks before that any questions arise or any creative and dramatic play indicate that the experience has been absorbed.

INSIDE THE NURSERY

Cookery

In these days of convenience foods, frozen vegetables and packeted desserts, fewer children are given the chance to see vegetables, meat and fish in their raw state and learn how they are prepared and cooked for us to eat. Home baking is not so common now that cakes and biscuits are selected from the supermarket shelf. Cookery in the nursery supervised by an adult will allow young children to take part in preparation, mixing and cooking of different foods, to see what happens when ingredients are mixed together, to develop fine motor skills when weighing, pouring, cutting and cracking eggs, to see what some of our foods are made of and to learn something about the effects of heating substances. This then is a discovery activity in its truest sense.

Many children today when asked will say that peas and beans originate from tins or the freezer. A visit to the greengrocers and the chance to grow vegetables in the nursery garden will help them to learn about where these vegetables come from, and they also need to have the vegetables in front of them to wash off the garden soil, to shell the peas and shred the beans, feeling their crisp freshness and tasting them in their raw state. With the addition of some good stock (a large meat bone purchased from the butcher will provide great interest) vegetable soup may be made and eaten at dinner time.

Cakes, biscuits and pastries are always popular, but it is important to select recipes which allow each child to participate fully in the activity. Each child should be able to roll his own piece of pastry, to take part in adding the ingredients, beating them and placing them into cake cases. Some adults do find it difficult to stand back and only intervene when really necessary but unless they can do this the children will not be really involved or learning. A good recipe for individual cake making is as follows : for each child, one plastic cream cheese carton, one tsp. margarine, one tsp. castor sugar, one dessert sp. flour, one table sp. egg and milk mixed together. Each child can mix his ingredients in his tub and spoon out the mixture into his own cake cases which are then placed into a baking tray with his name on them. He can then take his own utensils and do his own washing up. Variations may be added to this recipe by allowing the children to choose cocoa, coconut, sultanas or nuts to add to their cake mixture.

Jam tarts are popular – each child can have his own piece of pastry with some flour. Jam fillings may be varied with cheese for cheese straws, sausages, and fruit. Bread making is not such an ambitious cookery activity as it sounds so long as there is sufficient time to allow the dough to prove. Each child will be delighted with his own bread roll at the end of the morning. Another group of children may be able to make butter by taking turns at shaking a screw topped jar half-filled with the cream from the top of the milk.

Sweet making could be specially kept for Christmas and Easter times. Coconut ice and fondant sweets are the simplest to make. Sugar mice are particularly attractive for the children to make from a stiff fondant mixture. Each child can have a small ball on a polystyrene dish and can choose silver balls, sultanas, smarties or chopped cherries for eyes and ears. Pieces of string or tiny pieces of liquorice are admirable for tails.

Cookery is both valuable and a delight for young children, but it is a more specific activity and can only accommodate so many children who should be encouraged to remain until they have completed their cooking. Numbers of children may be limited around the cookery table by only providing so many cookery aprons. Washing hands should be a regular habit before cooking starts. At first children will need considerable supervision, but after a few weeks of practice they will become rema.kably competent, and the adult will be present mainly to pinpoint exactly what is taking place during the mixing and cooking process. When basic recipes have been well tried a large scrap book can be kept to gather new recipes and children may be able to contribute to these from home.

The discovery corner
Sometimes a small area of the nursery may be known as the 'discovery' or 'experiment' corner. The children will soon get to know that this is where one or two items are placed each week for them to investigate, discuss with an adult and sometimes use to develop their fantasy play. It is presumptuous to call this investigation 'science' but the foundations of scientific discovery are being laid. The following are a few examples of equipment to provide:

a An old television or radio with tube and valves removed and a series of screwdrivers.

b A collection of magnets of varying strengths and a selection of wooden, plastic and metal objects for 'testing'.

c A box of assorted plugs and screwdrivers.

d A selection of padlocks and different keys.

e Insides of clocks and watches and screwdrivers.

f Nuts and bolts in varying sizes.

g Torches with and without batteries.

Discovery situations may of course take place in any part of the nursery. Experiments with icecubes melting in warm and cold water, substances that dissolve in water, lighting bonfires in the ga:den and seeing materials burn and examining the ashes afterwards, seeing what things fly in the air: all this investigation will be feeding a child's curiosity.

Interest tables

We have already discussed interest tables and sensory discrimination. Further displays may be set up as a result of the investigations outlined above. If a child tests what articles can fly in the air, and then with the aid of the adult he sets up a table grouping his findings it will help to clarify the discovery in his own mind, and he can reinforce his findings by looking for suitable pictures of aeroplanes, kites and birds to add to the display.

Literature

Some children will come to the nursery having had no experience of stories, and therefore with no idea of the need within themselves to look at books or to listen to an adult reading to them. These children should be led gently into the world of literature on a one to one basis with an adult, although group story time should remain voluntary. If large compulsory story groups are established at this age, particularly with an indifferent story teller, there is a real danger of at least some of the children becoming adept at sitting quietly and 'switching off'. Small children need a rich diet of picture and story books presented to them in small groups, where at least some of them can have physical contact with the adult reading. If we are to be successful in motivating a child to want to learn to read later on, and to gradually build up a love and appreciation of literature, he must from the earliest age learn to look upon stories as a pleasurable experience. For more fortunate children initial experiences of hearing a story will be with a parent in a warm sharing relationship: other children may only have received their stories through the medium of the television, where if they are sitting alone they can only passively receive the material (anyone who has read or told stories to small children knows that interruption, discussion and elaboration are an integral part of the story). The teacher then needs to be aware of which individuals still need an introduction to books through this physical relationship, and those children whose experience is sound enough to enable them to be ready for group stories.

Any teacher of young children when looking to her requirements will surely consider books as of primary importance, but perhaps it is worthwhile to consider for a moment just what benefits we hope that a young child will derive from a well stocked and frequently replenished book corner.

Stories can be an important means of enabling a child to come to terms with a new or difficult situation in his life. The coming of a new baby, accepting the fact of being adopted, going to a new school or learning about the death of a grandparent can all be traumatic incidents for a small child who has still very limited experience on which to draw. Situation story books then can introduce the situation to the child and by showing how the character in the book deals with it can sometimes offer positive help to a child who is attempting to cope with a similar experience. Apart from this books will generally aid a child to understand and accept experiences and behaviour that he is faced with in daily situations. If he hears about other children who have temper tantrums and have angry parents and he also listens to the end of the story where the temper is over and is followed by love and affection, this can be reassuring when he is still at the stage of unstable emotions and fear of having affection withdrawn.

Stories, poetry and rhymes all create a sound foundation for children's language development. Varied stories will enable the children to become conversant with different styles of language and rhythm, new vocabulary will be introduced, and eventually after hearing a loved story again and again, the child will be able to recount it in his own words emphasizing those incidents which have had the most meaning for him.

Sybil Marshall aptly describes the way books foster the growth of the imagination:

By the magic of words and pictures, experiences of people, places and things lying outside the normal activities and environment of children can be brought close to them, and situations outside the arbitrary limits of their space and time can be presented to them for their inspection and assessment, in order that their insatiable curiosity may be satisfied. (Cass, 1967, Introduction)

Most successful stories for nursery children do require some element of realism about them however – total suspension of disbelief is very difficult for a young child if it is something of which he has no comprehension.

Finally, books will help to satisfy a desire for factual knowledge, but for these facts to have the greatest impact on the young child the book should follow the experience. Until a child can have the sensory experience of feeling and holding a rabbit, a book about the habits of this animal will be relatively meaningless.

If these are the main benefits of books and stories, what types of literature should be provided in the nursery? In view of the ever increasing wealth of children's books appearing in the shops today it is not possible to give a helpful and comprehensive list of their titles, but only to suggest the main categories. Situation books have already been mentioned, dealing simply and sensitively with the particular experiences common to a child. There has always been the firm belief that children under five should not be given stories about the supernatural as they are not yet able to separate fact from fiction. The effect of the mass media does sometimes mean that children are now more sophisticated in their tastes and do in fact enjoy the vicarious thrill of the traditional fairy tale or simple folk tale. Although the bulk of nursery stories will still be within the realm of everyday life, I suggest that there is now a place for magical fantasy, and even an element of fear in stories so long as the ending is completely reassuring.

Cardboard books and those with large colourful pictures and little text should be available for the youngest children. Again a variety of pictorial styles should be available, and also different sizes of books for the child to learn to handle. As the child matures he is able to rely less and less on the visual aspect of the story and pay attention to the content, until he comes to the stage of being able to listen to a story without pictures.

Telling stories to children does require a certain expertise, and some new teachers do lack the confidence not to rely on a book. However if they select the right material and make sure that the story is suitable in length – about five or six minutes is about right – then all that remains is to make themselves completely familiar with the story. The fact of being in direct contact with the children often makes it easier for the teacher to assess their mood and response when she can react accordingly. Occasionally stories may be told with the aid of visual props. A puppet, or an article drawn out of a bag will add interest to the story content particularly for those children who still need to rely more on visual impact. Other sensory material may also be introduced such as suitable sound effects or an interesting textured material which is mentioned in the story.

Reference books for young children need to be simple, accurate and brightly coloured. Text should be kept to a minimum and the pictures as far as possible self-explanatory in order for the children to use them as and when they need them without always having to ask for adult interpretations.

Children will use books in many ways: they will sit in the book corner, or sometimes in a comfortable chair provided in the home corner just browsing and tasting the delights of pictures. They will have stories individually and in groups, and will learn to go to books for specific information. The teacher's task is to make sure that all these book facilities are provided, and – also very important – that each book is selected carefully for quality and content. As Joan Cass rightly says:

It is important to remember that children are not born with inherent good taste. Left entirely to their own devices with such an enormous number of books available, they can waste a great deal of time on very mediocre material. Childhood does not last for ever, and if a book is not discovered at the appropriate stage it may never be read or seen at all.

Music

The fortunate child whose first experience of a story is on his parent's
knee will also have his first introductions to music through early
lullabies from his mother. Listening to music is primarily an emotional
experience, but we use the term 'music' loosely to include all nursery
activity which involves rhythm, movement, drama melody and
rhymes. Some children of three and four may have had little or no
experience of any of this activity and their introduction to it needs to
be gradual and in stages. The music session should be short and
voluntary and initially very simple. The first session could in fact omit
the music altogether, and concentrate on encouraging the children
to build up an awareness of their own bodies. Discovering feet,
shoulders, and noses can be great fun and the children can
experiment just what they can do with parts of their bodies. Later,
suitable taped music can provide opportunities for large muscle action
such as skipping, hopping and running. When the children really
become adept at these various movements and are able to change
from one to the other, they may like to try various dramatic
interpretations to the music: trees swaying, running down a winding
path, snakes wriggling in the grass – there are endless possibilities,
but it is important to remember that the interpretation is for each child
to decide, and the 'we all do it like this' technique will nullify any
creativity in the activity.

Musical instruments for young children should be limited to rhythm
and pitched percussion. The four basic rhythm instruments are drums,
bells, scrapers and shakers. Through using these instruments the
children will learn to discriminate between quick and slow beats and
loud and soft effects. After using these he may be introduced to
pitch by experimenting with simple glockenspiels and chime bars,
with bottles filled with different levels of water, with home-made
guitars constructed from a shoe box and different lengths of rubber
band. Most of these instruments can be made successfully, often
with the aid of the children. The instruments should be used
occasionally in a structured situation with a group of children
learning the names of instruments and listening to the different
sounds that they make, but there also should be plenty of opportunity
for the child to have access to a 'sounds' table where he may
experiment freely with various noises. It is also a good idea
occasionally to limit the types of sounds, by just displaying a selection
of drums or bells. Again the children should have practice in starting
and stopping their instruments and this may be done by encouraging
them to play with a record or with the aid of a piano.

Live music can be a great experience for children and therefore any
adult who is willing to visit the nursery to play an instrument very
briefly and then show the group just where the music comes from,

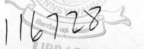

121

will be very welcome. To watch a saxophone in action or to gaze at the vast size of a double bass and listen to its growly sounds will have ten times the effect of any taped or recorded music. It should be emphasized however that a teacher does not have to be a music expert, or able to play an instrument in order to take a successful music session with young children. Her main quality should be enthusiasm and lack of self-consciousness, and a clear singing voice is an asset. Songs and rhymes should form a large part of any nursery programme and need not be kept for a music session. Children can be encouraged to sing spontaneously in a group and to build up a large repertoire of songs, some of them with actions. Singing games may also be introduced, although the children will only gradually learn to move in a group.

Finally, there will be occasions on a hot day, or after an exhausting activity or when it is wet and the children are fretful, when music can be used in a purely therapeutic way. Suitable records should be on hand for quiet listening or as a tranquil background for painting and creative activity.

The main principle with music, as with all other activities, is to provide as wide a range of experience for the child as possible whilst keeping it relevant to his stage of development. (A list of suitable records and music books for young children is supplied in Appendix D.)

7
Creating the environment

Our aim in part 2 has been to see how a nursery unit works in terms of activities and how these activities meet the needs of the child. In our first section we looked at the developing child and saw what does take place in the years between two and five. A purely descriptive section listed the main curricula which may stabilize and extend these facets of development. However, it would be misleading even to suggest that, given these suggested materials and activities, the ideal nursery environment will magically appear: it can only ultimately disillusion the new teacher to believe this, and those with experience will know only too well that other requirements are necessary. These requirements, we suggest, are as follows: knowing and understanding the children; knowing and understanding the child's home environment; organizing time in the nursery; organizing materials in the nursery; considering the teacher's role. Each of these requirements will be discussed in more detail in this final chapter.

KNOWING AND UNDERSTANDING THE CHILDREN
This requirement is not confined to nursery teachers — it applies to anyone in a teaching situation, but it is crucial to success with small children, and it cannot be acquired instantly. If any rapport is to be developed between adult and child in the nursery, the teacher must have an intimate knowledge of how that child functions — she should learn when to anticipate temper tantrums, and what provokes them, and to understand when a child is over-excited and noisy what is the most effective way of calming him — when to expect a child to be capable of coping with a group situation and what activities to lay out for him to best promote his development. Two types of knowledge are required — the first comes with sheer experience of dealing with many small children — fundamental patterns are seen to develop, and the experienced teacher, like the experienced mother, will act almost instinctively. Secondly, both the new and experienced teacher need a sound foundation of child development and to apply this knowledge to each individual child. This is important in all stages of schooling, but at three and four years a child needs an adult around, both at

home and in his pre-school setting, who is familiar to him and whom he knows understands his particular needs.

Once the teacher and child have successfully formed a sound relationship, and the child has become sure of his surroundings, then the benefits of being in his new environment should be seen. Gradually, by investigation and experimentation with materials, and interaction with his peers, the child will develop new skills, and with the aid of his teacher will be motivated to look for further dimensions in his learning.

Total experience in the nursery should serve to aid the child towards a more independent attitude to life. We have seen in our section on development how all small children are by definition dependent, and depending on both genetic and environmental influences some are more dependent than others. By gently easing the child into a situation outside his home which is specifically designed to promote his growth, we should be helping the child to overcome his fears, to gain confidence and to unfold as he gains the incentive to act freely.

Independence however has many connotations, particularly as the teacher views it in the young child — it can mean anything from social adeptness to going to the lavatory unaided. Whilst recognizing that all endeavours to aid a child's self sufficiency are laudable, Leslie Webb (1974) suggests that there is a deeper and more complex type of independence which we should consider as nursery teachers:

It is an easy matter to approve of such a contribution when the self-reliance engendered is in the matter of doing up buttons, washing, toileting and eating properly at table . . . . All these things help adults who are pressed for time, whether as parents or as teachers of large groups. Much more controversial . . . are emotional and intellectual independence. These are probably far more crucial to children's futures than independence in other areas, and it is precisely in encouraging rational, personal autonomy (i.e. the ability of a young child to think for himself) that the Nursery School or Class has its most important function.

This is the most difficult task of all for the nursery teacher and yet we would agree that this is of paramount importance to the child. Success in attaining this form of independence depends on the carefully planned nursery, but above all it depends upon the teacher knowing the individual child, his strengths and weaknesses and helping him to be himself.

This is a practical book however and we recognize that there are real difficulties to working meaningfully with children individually with a staff ratio of 1 :10 or, in nursery classes, 1 :13. Some suggestions to help overcome this are in the sections on organizing time and materials.

124

Knowing and understanding the child's home environment

Commonsense, backed by modern research, has shown that a child does not enter a nursery unmarked by previous experience (see chapter 3). His home and local environment have already played a great part in his formative years and despite the time spent in a nursery will continue to do so. The family must be considered to be the prime educative influence for the child – if we honestly recognize this then the implications of our aiding the child towards emotional and intellectual independence become even greater, particularly with the child living in disadvantaged circumstances. It is no earthly good a nursery teacher trying to mould a child into an image which she considers will be beneficial for him. If the home environment differs vastly from the middle-class ethos (which it still is) of the nursery then the child is inevitably in a conflict situation by being confronted by two modes of life. One mode may be pleasanter and considered 'better' for him – the other mode will have the final say in his future. The only way open to the nursery teacher is to attempt to foster the child's developing self, and secondly to do all she can to bridge the gap between home and school – it may be unrealistic even to suggest that the gap can be narrowed, but if the beginning of a mutual understanding and respect can be achieved, then there is meeting ground for both parties.

Knowing the family background therefore involves a great deal more than accumulating facts on paper about the number and age of siblings and occupation of the father. It involves working with the parents right from the beginning as described in the steps for a child entering a nursery, and then attempting to develop an ongoing relationship. The parent above all else must somehow be made aware of his own crucial role in his child's present and future, whilst gently being assured of support from nursery staff. The word *support* is an important one – we would like to refute any idea that the nursery unit supports a professional takeover bid, leaving the parent devoid of responsibility and reward. The nursery can only be a back-up system, and how effective it is as a back-up will depend on its success in working with the child's parents as well as the child. This is not the place to discuss in detail how school/home relationships are to be developed (see chapter 3) but to make clear that this is a large part of the teacher's task in creating a successful nursery environment. Homes are different and parents in different communities will vary in attitudes. The advantaged child will have parents who have already laid sound foundations and who will wish to be involved with the teacher in helping the nursery to be an extension of their home. Other parents will have unhappy experiences of their own schooldays and be unsure of their standing as parents – a warm introduction for them and their child to the nursery may help balance previous prejudice and reassure them of their role. Finally, some parents are beset by social difficulties so acute that their time and energy is spent trying to exist, and they cannot even contemplate interesting themselves in their children's schooling. This presents the greatest challenge to the teacher, and it must be admitted that, as both Willem Van Der Eyken and Eric Midwinter suggest, the state nursery unit may not be the best type of pre-school provision for this sector of the community — we are after all an institution, albeit an attractive one, and these parents are often unable to take advantage of anything organized or involving a group situation. However, until Willem Van Der Eyken's 'comprehensive policy of pre-schooling which seeks to intervene in the social matrix and to benefit the entire population of under-fives within its purview' is achieved, many areas will be asking existing nursery units and playgrounds to make provision for their most socially deprived children. In this case it may well be that authorities must be persuaded to provide transport to collect pre-school children to attend nursery units (many parents will not be prepared to bring and collect them) and for the nursery teacher to be given time to visit these homes with the specific intention of rekindling the parent's interest and involvement in his child. These provisions are of course part of the community nursery unit policy which is dealt with elsewhere in this book.

ORGANIZATION

Organizing time in the nursery

Time is one of the precious commodities awaiting the child entering the nursery. He is often deprived of long stretches at home — all too often his time is interrupted to be rushed into outdoor clothes to accompany mother to do the morning shopping: on his return he may be moved from room to room as the house is being cleaned, and then rushed into clothes again to be taken to meet his older brothers and sisters from school. These outings can be made pleasurable experiences, but more often they are hurried moments in the day as his busy mother attempts to cram them in to an already over full programme. Or there is the other child who is abandoned to time and the telly — noise is restricted because of complaining neighbours — his mother is too depressed or apathetic to join in his activities and he has no playmates. This child may spend his time in a fixed stupor in front of a moving screen, alternating with bursts of hyper-activity which are hushed by alternate bribes and punishments. Other children may be more fortunate, but all children need uninterrupted time in which to develop their growth play and this should be the teacher's first concern when planning her day. After marking out pivots of time which may be for eating, washing and small group or individual sessions with children, the remainder of a nursery day should be devoted to free choice of play, indoor or out, amidst a variety of materials and activities.

The extremes of the day are vulnerable times for a child — at the beginning of the session he is bidding farewell to his mother and sometimes a little reluctant or, more often, keyed up in anticipation of the day ahead. When collected by his parent he is tired, full up with experiences, sometimes unwilling to leave his peers at the nursery and occasionally relieved and comforted to see his mother or father if he has had a fall or an argument with a friend at school. At these times the teacher should be available to him — to greet him in the morning and to make him feel that she is personally pleased to see him arrive, and to say goodbye at the end of the session when he prepares to go home. These are busy times for the teacher, although by allowing arrival and departure time to extend over half an hour she should attempt to make these comfortable periods for having a word of greeting for each child and at least a few moments for any parent who wishes to talk.

A nursery teacher does not have a leisurely day — but in order to achieve a successful nursery routine she must somehow make it a leisurely one for the children and most of all conserve her energies for them and their parents. She will need to make the fullest use of all other adults working in the nursery during that session — truly a successful partnership between the teacher and nursery nurse is called for, and any parents or students should be requested to work with certain groups of children or in certain activity areas to allow the teacher's time to be deployed with a selected group or individual who needs specific help.

If one of our aims in the nursery is to help the young child to become a self-regulating creature it will not assist him if we chop his day up into small segments regulating when he needs to go to the lavatory and how much milk he requires to drink. Clearly a careful eye must be kept on newcomers, but most children will instinctively rest after an active period of play, and with an occasional reminder for the individual, they will visit the lavatory when they feel the need and be more relaxed about it because there is no need to hurry or queue. A mid-morning snack need not be an elaborate time-consuming affair. If the children learn that they can help themselves from a table and pour their own amount of milk they will go when they are thirsty, and when a natural break occurs in their activity. The main meal of the day does need to be a group occasion and is an important social event when small groups of children can converse with an adult, acquire social eating habits and generally attain a family-like intimacy. Most children will not require to sleep after the midday meal, although a brief quiet spell with table toys or a story will aid their digestion before the pattern of play begins again.

In order to make provision for varied needs, most nursery units have an intake of morning, afternoon and full-day children. This means that the teacher's timetable has to be geared to the needs of both full and part-time children. She needs to bear in mind therefore the necessity to provide a balanced session for morning and afternoon children – both sessions should be similar in length and content – there should be opportunities for optional music and story sessions, and specific activities such as cookery or craft. However, exact repetition of the morning session in the afternoon may not stretch the full-time children sufficiently – their play should be allowed to continue throughout the day and if possible should not be started again 'cold' in the afternoon.

Organizing materials in the nursery

As we have mentioned, a nursery environment should provide for all the varying developmental needs of the child, and this is considered when planning what to set out each day, remembering that variety and further additions for development are needed. Broadly speaking, a nursery needs to make daily provision for some type of messy play, some painting activity and a range of construction toys and puzzles for selection, an area for building or woodwork, an imaginative play area with dressing up whether a hospital, home corner or shop, a nature area, book corner, interest or display area and a craft area for collage or junk modelling. Outside there will be various equipment to allow for physical outlets, for building, for messy play whether with mud or sand or both, for imaginative play in a den or old vehicle, an area for plants and animals and some outside seats to allow for quiet moments.

The room should look attractive and ready for the child, and it can only do so if it is prepared in advance. However, it is a mistake to hand over a ready-made environment to the child – the more he is involved with his situation, the better he gets to know his environment, including the planning of it, the better his chances of being self-reliant and seeing a pattern to his day. On his entry he can help to mix paints, fill water trays and collect cookery ingredients as needed. The getting out and putting away of materials at the end of the session should be part of the programme, but should not be so arduous as to interfere with actually using the materials.

The teacher will be greatly helped if she organizes herself to check equipment and materials methodically. Good stores of junk materials and collage need to be kept and sorted. Cutlery and cups and saucers in the home corner need checking as do dolls and miniature toys. Dressing up clothes should be clean and well presented, and sand and water equipment should be checked for missing articles and breakages. All this may be obvious but none the less important – the child's play will be affected by the state and quality of materials presented to him. Work done by the children should be hung around the room – it adds to the atmosphere of the child's environment and provides talking points. It is important to provide a balance here though – paintings and collages do need to be displayed attractively and with sensitivity: however as at this stage the child is more concerned with the activity rather than the finished product, the teacher will be advised to spend more of her time with the child than in hanging elaborate adult orientated designs on the walls. As much of the playroom as possible should belong to the children – they should be given the opportunity to display their work if they wish, and with the addition of a spirit gum they can easily attach their creations to the wall by themselves.

Finally, there should be a basic simplicity to the layout of equipment and materials in the room – children should be able to find what they want easily, and cope with as much as possible by themselves. A child should be able to enter the room, decide that he wishes to do some junk modelling, select an apron from a hook and put it on and fasten it himself. When he has made his model, he may wish to paint it and so moves to the painting area and afterwards places it on a low surface to dry – he can then go to wash his hands, remove his apron and hang it up and be ready for his next activity. All this he may do unaided and by having most of the room organized in this way children may freely pass from one type of play to another without unnecessary pause, and the teacher may be freed to devote her attentions to specific children.

THE ROLE OF THE TEACHER

We come now to the last of our requirements for a nursery environment – that is the part that the teacher herself plays in the nursery. We have already looked at many of her most important jobs – aiding the children in various facets of their growth, assisting their independence and extending their language abilities and consequent powers of thought. We require her to regard the child's home and his parents as important as the child himself and to work in varying ways to achieve some meaningful relationships with them and where necessary to help them establish a sense of their own worth. We also ask that she is an efficient workman on nursery premises – organizing her time and materials to the best effect for the children. Can there be anything else? We have not yet considered the growth of moral values in the young child and this is perhaps where the teacher's role is a crucial one and related more closely to her personal qualities than any other. Some children come to the nursery unit already practising gentleness, caring and a sense of responsibility – clearly this development is still patchy because of their immaturity, but with these children it is clear that foundations for a code of conduct have been laid at home. Others come from homes of varying social class but where the predominant philosophy is 'grab what you can whilst you can' and yet others come from backgrounds where their sole directive from parents since they were toddlers has been 'don't be naughty' (naughtiness to include 'naughty messiness' or 'naughty inconvenient behaviour'). All of these children will start their pre-schooling still in a very vulnerable state and extremely responsive to the adults who are caring for them.

It is not our intention to state here what is a 'right' and 'wrong' type of behaviour for our young children to acquire, but to emphasize the great responsibility that is laid upon the teacher in guiding their moral behaviour. Moreover, we do not believe that any teacher should be arrogant enough in her own ways of thinking to feel it incumbent upon herself to condition her children. 'Conditioning' implies an inflexible attitude which cannot be tolerated with young children. Clearly rules must be established to maintain the safety and wellbeing of the group – these rules must be firmly stated and equally firmly carried out. They need not be many and even the young child should soon recognize their necessity. Apart from this however the ball is then thrown firmly into the nursery teacher's court – just what practices does she consider worthwhile holding up for approval to her children and how does she do this? We can only suggest that she will do well to consider her every gesture and inflection of approval and disapproval – just why is she so pleased that Johnny has tidied up the bricks – is it because he 'did as he was told' and the tidiness of the room pleases her, or is it because he gave her a smile as he did so and appears to be absorbed in the tidying up process? We further suggest that unless these rules have clear relevance for the teacher there is little chance of them appearing sensible to the child, and even if the teacher does see the underlying reason for the rule, the child may not yet have reached that stage of development where he is capable of appreciating it – this must be respected and understood by the teacher.

Finally, just how does the teacher reinforce those qualities in children that she believes to be worthwhile. As most of these young children are still very much at the imitative stage of development her methods will primarily be successful if she demonstrates by example. Consistent courtesy, honesty and an ability to laugh at her own mistakes will at least be a model for her children, and if the teacher retains a questioning attitude towards her own values then this will safeguard her against imposing doctrinaire views upon immature children.

In looking at the necessary requirements for establishing a thriving nursery environment, clearly the personnel play an important part in determining its success. Such qualities as we have outlined in this last section do depend on the existence of a high quality person who has received a sound and relevant training for her role. She also needs to be given time in a nursery before her talents are fully felt – a young newly trained teacher may well find that relating to the children and developing their cognition is within her scope, but gaining the confidence of parents and being able to work with a nursery assistant and students is something that will only come with added maturity. It is a responsibility to be a child's first teacher during his most formative years and we hope that more than lip service will be given to this responsibility in the future, both in terms of training, status and reward – only then will our young children receive the quality of nursery education that they deserve.

Conclusion

It has only been possible to touch upon the theory and practice of
Early Childhood Education in this book, but hopefully this will have
been enough to have stimulated the reader to think about what
provision is being made today. The few nursery schools that have
existed since the early part of this century have in the main to be
congratulated on preserving their child orientated environment, and
their frequent and easy contact with parents. New nursery schools and
classes have initiated more efficient organization, and are looking
critically at the child's cognitive development. Paper towels and
napkins have abolished the need for the weekly laundering chore,
record cards are being started at nursery level, and School Council
projects on pre-school language and mathematics are developing
with the aid of enthusiastic contributions from nursery staff. This is
the bright state of affairs: we can also say with truth that some of the
older nursery establishments are existing on the strength of tradition
only, and many new units have been placed into the hands of head
teachers who regard them as at best 'preparation classes for real
school'. Many nursery establishments, both old and new, still lack the
variety of informal contact with parents which is so important for the
young child's wellbeing, and are also failing to make their institution
a useful and workable part of the neighbourhood in which they are
situated. A combination of the best in traditional and modern nursery
practice is called for together with an approach to other community
agencies which exist to support the young child and his family today.

Appendix A

SUGGESTED ONE YEAR PROGRAMME FOR TRAINING THE NURSERY NURSE STUDENT IN THE PRACTICAL SITUATION

The programme is based on the first year student being in the nursery unit for two days a week for alternate weeks during three terms. It aims gradually to allow the student a degree of responsibility until she is a fully capable operator in the nursery field at the end of the year. The programme can clearly be adjusted to the needs of the more or less able student.

First term

1 Remembering that the student is entering a completely new training situation time should be given her to adapt to the environment, to see the daily timetable in action and as far as possible to get to know the children by name.

2 Aim to show the student the various materials used in the nursery, and demonstrate the most suitable methods for preparation and presentation of these materials, e.g. the water and sand tray – why particular equipment is used with this material; preparation of paint – mixing to the correct texture; recipe for finger paint; why we use large brushes and paper; care and presentation of clay and dough.

3 Domestic routine in the nursery. Daily cleaning of washbasins and lavatories; routine disinfecting procedures.

4 The daily setting out of the playroom – aim to show how and why a balance of activities is presented. Clearing away at the end of the day – need for careful maintenance of equipment, e.g. repairing books and mending toys.

5 Learning to relate to each individual child – the importance of a different approach to each must be emphasized as no two children are alike. Particular attention should be paid to children with special needs.

Second term

1 Student to be responsible for preparing, presenting and clearing away one creative activity a week with the children (including some cookery activity of their choice). This should give her the opportunity to try out any ideas suggested at college. Experimentation should be encouraged.

2 Student to be given responsibility for a story session with a small group of children (again she should be able to put into practice all the theory of presenting books suggested at college).

3 Opportunity for the student to have a regular rhythm and jingle session with a group of children. She should previously have acquired a good fund of finger rhymes and should now be capable of coping adequately with a small group situation.

Third term

1 Regular opportunity for the student to take voluntary music sessions with a group of children (simple dramatic play and movement included). This often requires a certain amount of confidence and is a more suitable aspect of training to leave until the latter part of the year.

2 Display and nature tables to be organized both with and without the children.

3 The second part of the third term should provide some chance for the student to show her ability in organizing and setting out the playroom as she requires, with the staff acting as assistants as far as possible.

NB This programme is intended to show the development of responsibility in training – throughout the year the student should have a daily routine of working as a member of the nursery team and being involved with all that that entails.

Appendix B

RECORD KEEPING

Why keep records?

Traditionally record keeping has not been considered relevant in the nursery sector save (in some cases) for health purposes. One reason for this is the smallness and intimacy of nursery units and the expectation that nursery teachers should know their children well enough without needing recourse to the written word: also the fact that much of what is being achieved with children at this level is difficult to define. There has also been the fear that by keeping records the spontaneity and non-competitive nature of the nursery would be lost to children being tested for levels of attainment which they will pass or fail. This is a reasonable fear, and any testing and recording which unduly distracts the child from his precious hours in the nursery and takes up too much time on the teacher's part is self-defeating. However, we suggest that it is important to keep records at nursery level for the following reasons:

1 To start building up a total picture of each child, and to ensure that satisfactory development has taken place during the years before statutory schooling begins.

2 To ascertain when development is not progressing normally, and to record when suitable remedial action is taken (e.g. child affected by home situation and health visitor or social worker informed).

3 To provide more continuity at First School level. The reception teacher in the First School should not start her work in a vacuum, but should continue with the child, fostering and extending the development that has previously taken place. Continuity is easier to achieve when nursery units are attached to First Schools; where nursery schools exist independently and serve a number of First Schools, written records become very important.

4 To record daily activity in the nursery, including particularly successful projects with children. It is useful for teachers to look back to see what they have achieved, and for students and visitors coming to the nursery to see what type of work is undertaken with this age group over a period.

Points to consider in keeping good records

1 They should be simple and mainly factual, although parents' opinions of their children are sometimes valuable.

2 Records should be capable of being understood by anyone having access to them.

3 Records should be cumulative and should be kept up to date.

4 The information should be pertinent and brief. Unnecessarily bulky records are inconvenient and record keeping should take up the minimum of time.

Types of records for the nursery with examples

Application form
This initial form should only request essential information from parents, but it is important that there is provision for a fairly full recommendation if the admission is to be considered a priority one. The information on the application form will form the start of the child's record.

Example

Green Lane Nursery School
Application form for admission

Name of Child :   Date of Birth :

Home Address :   Telephone Number :

I prefer am/pm admission :

I would like eventual full-time admission :

Please state reason for wanting nursery place for child :

Recommendation for admission : (this to be completed by social worker, doctor etc.)

Signature of parent :

Date of Application :

Parental profile of child

When the nursery teacher first visits the home, she can ask the parents to fill in further details about their child and family. Depending on the family she might leave the form or help the parents to complete the details, adding a few explanatory notes herself. This record can then be clipped to the initial application form to provide some picture of the home background.

Example

Green Lane Nursery School

Family Record

Name of Child: Family Doctor's address and Tel No:

Does your child enjoy good health?
(If no, please state weaknesses)

Does he suffer from any allergy?

Has he had all the necessary innoculations?

Father's place of work:

Mother's place of work (or where she is most likely to be contacted during the day):

Number and ages of children in family:

Has your child had the opportunity to mix with other children?

Please state your child's favourite activity at home:

Has he/she any particular fears?
(if so please give details)

Date of admission to nursery:

Developmental records whilst in the nursery

The nursery teacher is advised to have a loose leaf notepad permanently in her pocket with a page allotted for each child. As she works with small groups and individuals she is able to note aspects of development and date them. She should check that she has some comment for each child every week.

Example

1 Ann Smith 13.5.72 Mother admitted to hospital yesterday. Ann is very withdrawn and refuses to be parted from a woolly blanket.

2 John Brown 16.5.72 Maintained 12 min. conversation with two friends whilst using funnels and containers in the dry sand tray : now fully aware of the following concepts — full, empty, half-full.

At the end of every term, the teacher can read through these jottings and from this she should be able to note some pattern of development. This summary can then be noted permanently in the record file (together with some samples of the child's work).

Example

Developmental Record

Name of Child : Ann Smith   Date of Birth : 6.4.69

Date of admission : 7.2.72

Autumn Term Report Mother has mentioned marital stress at home, but Ann seems unaffected and is happily settled in the nursery. She plays mostly in the home corner by herself, unable to join a group situation as yet, but enjoys individual stories. Shows a present left handed dominance.

Spring Term 1973 Ann is much more socially adept — now plays happily in a group. Paintings are representational (sample enclosed). Use of language is well developed — able to retell several short stories completely in sequence.

Final Report for First School
The final record in the nursery is when the child is about to transfer
to the First School, and the reception teacher needs this report to
give her an up-to-date picture of the individual, and to enable her to
anticipate his next stage of development. This record can be added
to the others as a final summary of development during the nursery
years. The entire dossier including any reports from doctors or other
agencies should then be passed on to the First School.

Example

Green Lane Nursery School
Record Summary for First School

Name: Ann Smith   Date of Record: 8.4.74

Any specific change in family circumstances since initial record:
  Parents recently separated: child not unduly disturbed and is now
  living with mother who is working full time.

Social and emotional development
A very stable child – usually leads a group. Confident and independent
with her peers and with adults.

Physical development
Slightly short sighted (see enclosed medical report).
Enjoys large apparatus and is agile and has well developed physical
skills.
Her finer manipulative movements are slightly clumsy (possibly due to
short-sightedness). Uses scissors and glues competently. Left handed
dominance.

Cognitive development
Language – uses language to reason and analyse: uses an elaborated
code: good vocabulary: can match words.
Mathematics – good mathematical vocabulary: can match by colour
and shape. Counts to 20 and matches one to one up to ten: good
spatial awareness.
Favourite present activity: domestic play and outside activity.
Any other relevant information: Ann has coped remarkably well with
an unstable family background. Father has played little part in her
life, but mother has continued to foster her development in the best
possible way.

Activity in the Nursery Unit

The nursery teacher needs to provide herself with a rough framework of activity prepared in advance. However, as the essence of a nursery programme is its spontaneity, the permanent record should be completed at the end of each week after the activity has taken place. These records are meant to be very brief with occasional mention of particular successful responses and failures. Occasionally there is a place for a more detailed analysis of a particular project (see Parry and Archer 1974) but this is time consuming and not practicable as a regular feature if the teacher is to complete her individual records.

Example

Activity Record

Week ending 5th May   Theme: Vegetables

Monday Cabbage for children to dissect – caterpillars found and put in jar on nature table. Picture of allotment with small group discussion (great interest shown as many children had fathers who grew vegetables). Vegetable bed outside weeded and dug.

Other Activities Woodwork outside: floating and sinking objects in waterplay: painting easel, children mixed their own paint.

Tuesday Examination of vegetables with roots using knives and magnifying glass.
Cookery – washing and preparing vegetables and preparing soup. Planting beans and peas and carrots in the garden. Story: 'The enormous turnip'.

Other activities Dry sand, clay, dolls house, painting easels.

Appendix C

SOME ACTIVITIES AND ASSOCIATED SKILLS

Waterplay

Tipping and pouring
Equipment: jugs, bottles, tubes, funnels, water wheel, teapot.
Floating and sinking objects
Equipment: two different coloured containers where floating or sinking objects may be placed after being tested. A selection of varied materials e.g. feathers, matchboxes, marbles, buttons. A selection of objects that look similar but that react differently e.g. golf ball, ping pong ball, plastic spoon, metal spoon.
What holds water
Equipment: tea strainer, colander, sieve, metal spoon, metal spoon with holes, plastic bottles with and without holes of varying sizes, absorbent and non-absorbent papers and cloths.
Making bubbles (comparing sizes, shape and colour)
Equipment: plastic bubble pipes or metal loops, washing-up liquid, glycerine to add colour to bubbles.
Washing clothes (water and soap remove dirt and create bubbles)
Washing dolls (imaginative home play)
Equipment: towels, soap, talcum powder.
Fishing (use of a magnet in water)
Equipment: fish cut out from thin plastic or rubber or pieces of wood and fixed with paper clips. Water coloured with sea green crêpe paper, sea shells for decoration, wooden doweling fishing rods with small magnets attached.
Water is colourless and takes on whatever colour that is added to it
Equipment: A tank of clear water and pieces of different coloured crêpe paper to add to the water (as the paper is added the colour will flow into the water and diffuse).
Sailing boats (floating and sinking experiments, and imaginative play)
Equipment: commercially produced and home made boats of plastic, wood and paper of varying types and sizes.

Sand: Dry

Tipping and pouring
Equipment: as with water.
Size of grains
Equipment: a variety of different meshes to sift the grains, a magnifying glass.
Volume
Equipment: jugs and measures of graded sizes.
'Drawing'
Equipment: a thin layer of dry sand, the children's fingers or pointed sticks for pattern making, a 'rubber' in the form of a flat piece of wood.

Sand: Wet

Moulding
Equipment: small buckets, plastic pots, jelly moulds and commercial shapes.
Pattern making
Equipment: wooden rakes, large plastic combs and sticks.
Imaginative play
Equipment: miniature vehicles, small soldiers, farm and zoo animals, pebbles, twigs.

Dough

Mixing dough (messy activity and substitute for cooking)
Place ingredients for making dough (see p 87) on the table and allow the children to add coloured water until the right consistency is obtained.
Sensory experiences from dough play
Visual – the children will learn to vary the amount and type of colouring additive to obtain different shades of coloured dough.
Tactile – different recipes for dough may be made up (see p 87) and compared.
Olfactory – different perfumes may be added to the dough mixture.
Print making (comparison of shape and size, pattern making)
Equipment: a series of objects with interesting textures to press into dough and leave their imprint e.g. buttons, shells, twigs.
'Cookery' (manipulation, domestic imaginative play, discovery of what happens to dough when it is cooked)
Equipment: small pastry cutters, blunt knives, bun tins. After the children have made their cakes they may be cooked in the oven and sometimes painted or varnished to use as pretend food in the home corner.
Stabiles (creative and manipulative play)

Equipment: stale dough to use as a base, individual pieces of cardboard or polystyrene dishes, a selection of milk tops, pipe cleaners, shells, stones, buttons, straws. Each child may make his own stabile by placing a piece of dough onto his cardboard or dish and arranging a series of objects in the dough.

Painting

Finger painting
Equipment: see main text p 91.
Printing
Equipment: for different types of prints:

a Handprints and footprints (have a bowl of soapy water nearby).

b Fruit and vegetable prints (merely cut them in half to retain their natural shape).

c Selection of different small junk shapes e.g. yoghourt pots, match boxes.

d Kitchen equipment e.g. pastry cutters, food whisks, forks.

e Small pieces of synthetic and natural sponge.
Comb patterns
Equipment: finger paint, cardboard or plastic combs to trace patterns in the paint. Organize this on a formica surface rather than on paper.
String painting
Equipment: various pieces of string of differing thicknesses and about 25cm (10″) in length, containers of medium thick paint.
Method: dip the string into the paint and lay on one side of a piece of paper. Fold the paper in half on top of the string and press down firmly. Pull the string out through the folded paper. Open up the paper to find a symmetrical print.
Wax painting
Equipment: wax candles or wax crayons, containers of very thin paint.
Method: use a piece of wax candle to draw an 'invisible' pattern over a piece of paper. Wash over the picture with very thin paint, and see the wax outline emerge.
Marbling
Equipment: shallow tin tray or dish, cooking oil or turpentine, powder paint, water, absorbent newsprint or blotting paper cut into small squares or shapes.
Method: mix the cooking oil or turps and powder paint together to provide a convenient and cheap oil paint. Mix two or three colours in different containers. Half fill the shallow container with water and place on the table: with a teaspoon gently pour a few drops of oil

paint onto the water. The oil will then diffuse and float, and the children will be absorbed watching the different oily patterns made on the water.

A print may then be taken by laying a sheet of paper over the tray for a few moments to absorb the colours, and then laying it flat to dry. (This activity is more suitable for older pre-school children when they start to look for an 'end product'. The younger children should be allowed to experiment freely with the oil paint and water with no emphasis on print taking.)

Straw painting

Equipment: two saucers of thin paint, each with a teaspoon: drinking straws cut into various lengths: strong paper.

Method: spoon a small amount of paint onto the paper, and then using a straw blow it in various directions.

Bubble prints

Equipment: round tin lids or saucers: washing-up liquid: powder paint: drinking straws: small squares of newsprint or other absorbent paper for taking prints.

Method: mix washing-up liquid and water in equal parts and add powder paint to colour. Pour some of the paint mixture into the tin lid and offer to the child with a drinking straw for him to blow bubbles. This should produce a mass of frothy, coloured bubbles and is in itself an absorbing game. When the child is ready a print can then be taken by placing a piece of newsprint over the bubbles and lifting it to dry.

Appendix D

SOME USEFUL BOOKS AND RECORDS TO USE WHEN MAKING MUSIC WITH YOUNG CHILDREN

Records for listening and moving

Young children find it difficult to sit still and listen to music, initially music is only meaningful to them if they can interpret it with body movement. Later, however, carefully selected short passages may be used when small groups are encouraged to sit or lie on the floor and listen. The following records may be used for both purposes (but only in short extracts).

Peter and the Wolf: Prokofiev
The Toy Symphony: Haydn
The Planets: Holst
The Nutcracker Suite: Tchaikovsky
Listen, Move and Dance I and II EMI 7EG8728/8
Listen, Move and Dance III Electronic EMI 7EG8762
Listen, Move and Dance IV Percussion EMI CLP 3531

Sound effects

Wind HMV 7FX10
Sea HMV 75X6
Rain and Ships HMV 75X7

Records of songs, rhymes and singing games

Children's Favourites MFP 1175
Play Songs (arranged by Avril Dankworth) Jupiter JEP OC40
Fingerplay Songs for the Nursery Paxton EEP 507
Simple Activity Songs for the Nursery Paxton EEP 514
Play Away BBC Records
Eight Ring Singing Games Paxton EEP 530
Action Rhymes Kids–6–301 Three–four–five Ltd.

Music and song books

Gobble, Growl and Grunt by Peter Spier. World's Work, 1972
Games and Songs of American Children by William Newall. Dover paperbacks
The Oxford Nursery Song Book compiled by P. Buck. Oxford University Press
Thirty Songs for the Nursery and Infant School compiled by W. E. Houghton. Boosey and Hawkes, 1943
Up and Doing for Nursery and Infant Classes by Dorothy Parr. Boosey and Hawkes, 1958
Music for the Nursery School by L. Chesterman. Harrap, 1944
What the Children Sing by A. Moffat. Stainer and Bell (Galliard), various editions
Singing Fun by Lucille Wood and L. B. Scott. Harrap, various editions

General books

Making Musical Apparatus and Instruments by K. Blocksidge. British Association for Early Childhood Education
My Kind of Music by Margaret Shephard. P.P.A. Publications
The Ladybird Book of Musical Instruments

Appendix E

SOME USEFUL ADDRESSES

These addresses have been compiled with the intention of providing easy access to reference sources. Group A are those organizations which will advise on the practicalities of pre-school provision, and also seek to expand this provision in varying ways. The addresses in Group B will give information on specific handicaps and also send details of local branches of these societies which exist throughout the country: parents of handicapped children often gain a great deal by being in touch with these societies. Group C are the organizations which take an interest in young children and their families as part of a more general social policy. The professional adult or playgroup supervisor may find it useful to seek advice herself or put families in touch with these bodies. Assistance may be given through informative literature, speakers provided at meetings, or in the case of individual family problems social workers may be able to visit and give help in their particular field.

A

The British Association for Early Childhood Education: Montgomery Hall, Kennington Oval, London SE11 5SW
(Publishes information on all aspects of nursery education.)
Pre-School Playgroups Association: Alford House, Aveline Street, London SE11 5DJ
(The National Association of Playgroups. An articulate pressure group aiming to provide a service for young children and their families. Publishes very useful booklets on all aspects of playgroup work.)
The Advisory Centre for Education (ACE): 32 Trumpington Street, Cambridge CB2 1QY
(A centre for information on education. Publishes the magazine *Where*.)

B

The Spastics Society: 12 Park Crescent, London W1

Association for all Speech Impaired Children: 9 Desenfans Road, Dulwich Village, London SE21

National Association for Mental Health: 39 Queen Anne Street, London W1

Association for Spina Bifida and Hydrocephalus: 112 City Road, London EC1

National Society for Autistic Children: 1a Golders Green Road, London NW11 8EA

National Elfrida Rathbone Society (educationally subnormal children): 17 Victoria Park Square, Bethnal Green, London E2

National Association for Deaf, Blind and Rubella Children: 33 Offerton Road, Hazel Grove, Stockport

The British Epilepsy Association: 3–6 Alfred Place, London WC1E 7ED

The above societies will provide information and support for families of children with these handicaps.

C

Save the Children Fund: 157 Clapham Road, London SW9
(Part of its work involves setting up playgroups in hospitals and socially deprived areas.)

National Children's Bureau: Adams House, 1 Fitzroy Square, London W1P 5AH
(An indepedent, interdisciplinary body catering for the needs of children of all ages.)

National Society for Prevention of Cruelty to Children: 1 Riding House Street, London W1P 8AA

Association of British Adoption Agencies: 4 Southampton Row, London WC1
(Provides practical advice on adoption and fostering.)

Gingerbread: 9 Poland Street, London W1
(A series of self-help single parent groups established throughout the country.)

National Council for One-Parent families: 255 Kentish Town Road, London NW5

National Association of Working Mothers: 28 Grange Road, London N6

National Association for Maternity and Child Welfare: BMA House, Tavistock Square, London WC1

National Council of Social Services: 26 Bedford Square, London WC1

Child Poverty Action Group: 1 Macklin Street, London WC1

Dr Barnardo's: Tanners Lane, Barkingside (Clevedon)

Family Planning Association: 27–35 Mortimer Street, London W1A 4QW

International Help for Children: 130 Eversholt Street, London NW1
Church of England Children's Society: Old Town Hall, Kennington
   Road, London SE11
Salvation Army International Headquarters: 101 Queen Victoria Street,
   London EC4

Bibliography

Allen of Hurtwood, Lady (1968) *Planning for Play*. Thames and
    Hudson.
Anderson, R.H. and H.G. Shane eds. (1971) *As the Twig is Bent*.
    Houghton Mifflin, Boston.
Ash, B., Winn, M. and K. Hutchinson (1971) *Discovering with Young
    Children*. Elek.
Banks, O. (1971) *The Sociology of Education*. Batsford.
Beadle, M. (1972) *A Child's Mind*. University Paperbacks.
Before Five (1971) Scottish Education Department. HMSO.
Bereiter, C. and S. Engelmann (1966) *Teaching Disadvantaged
    Children in the Pre-School*. Prentice-Hall, Englewood Cliffs.
Blackstone, T. (1971) *A Fair Start*. Allen Lane, The Penguin Press.
Cass, J.E. (1967) *Literature and the Young Child*. Longman.
Cass, J.E. (1971) *The Significance of Children's Play*. Batsford.
Cass, J.E. and D.E.M. Gardner (1965) *The Role of the Teacher in the
    Infant and Nursery School*. Pergamon.
Chazan, M. ed. (1973) *Education in the Early Years*. Faculty of
    Education, University College of Swansea.
Chazan, M. et al (1971) *Just before School*. Blackwell.
Crowe, B. (1973) *The Playgroup Movement*. George Allen and Unwin.
Davie, R., Butler, N. and H. Goldstein (1972) *From Birth to Seven*. A
    report of the National Child Development Study. Longman for the
    National Children's Bureau.
Dickinson, S. ed. (1972) *Mother's Help*. Collins.
Douglas, J.W.B. (1967) *The Home and the School*. Panther.
Education: a Framework for Expansion (1972) Cmnd 5174. HMSO
Erikson, E.H. (1965) *Childhood and Society*. Penguin Books.
Gesell, A. et al (1970) *The First Five Years of Life*. 4th ed. Methuen.
Gilbert, A. (1974) *Prime Time*. Evans.
Halsey, A.H. ed. (1972) *Educational Priority*, Volume I: E.P.A.
    Problems and Policies. HMSO.
Hurlock, E.B. (1972) *Child Development*. 5th ed. McGraw Hill.
Isaacs, S. (1954) *The Educational Value of the Nursery School*. U.L.P.

Jackson, B. and D. Marsden (1966) *Education and the Working Class*. Penguin Books.
Jameson, K. (1968) *Pre-School and Infant Art*. Studio Vista.
Jameson, K. and P. Kidd (1974) *Pre-School Play*. Studio Vista.
Kent, J. and P. (1970) *Nursery Schools for All*. Ward Lock Educational.
Kogan, M. and M. Pope eds. (1972) *The Challenge of Change*. National Foundation for Educational Research for the National Children's Bureau.
Lucas, J. and V. McKennell (1974) *The Penguin Book of Playgroups*. Penguin Books.
McGeeney, P. (1972) *Parents are Welcome*. Longman.
Mann, B.F. (1964) *Learning through Creative Work*. National Froebel Foundation.
Marshall, S. (1963) *An Experiment in Education*. Cambridge University Press.
Midwinter, E. ed. (1974) *Pre-School Priorities*. Ward Lock.
Molony, E. (1967) *How to form a Playgroup*. BBC.
Parry, M. and H. Archer (1974) *Pre-School Education*. Schools Council Research Studies. Macmillan.
Pines, M. (1969) *Revolution in Learning*. Allen Lane, The Penguin Press.
Pringle, M.L.K. (1974) *The Needs of Children*. Hutchinson.
Read, K. (1971) *The Nursery School*. W.B. Saunders.
Richmond, P.G. (1970) *An Introduction to Piaget*. Routledge and Kegan Paul.
Roberts, V. (1971) *Playing, Learning and Living*. A & C Black.
Schools Council (1972) *A Study of Nursery Education*. (Working paper 41) Evans/Methuen Educational.
Sheridan, M. (1968) *The Developmental Progress of Infants and Young Children*. Department of Health and Social Security.
Simms, J.A. and T.H. (1969) *From Three to Thirteen*. Longman
Tough, J. (1974) *Focus on Meaning*. Unwin Educational.
van der Eyken, W. (1974) *The Pre-School Years*. Penguin Books.
Wall, W.D. and V.P. Varma eds. (1972) *Advances in Educational Psychology*. U.L.P.
Webb, L. (1974) *Purpose and Practice in Nursery Education*. Blackwell.
Whitbread, N. (1972) *The Evolution of the Nursery-Infant School*. Routledge and Kegan Paul.
Williams, N. (1969) *Child Development*. Heinemann.
Winnicott, D.W. (1964) *The Child, The Family and the Outside World*. Penguin Books.
Wood, M.E. (1973) *Children: the Development of Personality and Behaviour*. Harrap.

Working Class Mothers and Pre-School Education (1972) East Newcastle Action Group.

Yardley, A. (1970) *Reaching Out*. Evans.

Yardley, A. (1970) *Senses and Sensitivity*. Evans.

Yardley, A. (1971) *The Teacher of Young Children*. Evans.